WORLD'S BEST CARD TRICKS

BOB LONGE

Sterling Publishing Co., Inc.   New York

In the Same Series

The World's Best Funny Rhymes
The World's Best Funny Songs
The World's Best Optical Illusions
The World's Best Party Games
The World's Best Puzzles
The World's Best Street & Yard Games
The World's Best String Games
The World's Best Travel Games
The World's Best "True" Ghost Stories
The World's Most Challenging Puzzles
The World's Strangest "True" Ghost Stories
The World's Toughest Puzzles
The World's Toughest Tongue Twisters

Library of Congress Cataloging-in-Publication Data

Longe, Bob, 1928-
    The world's best card tricks / by Bob Longe.
      p. cm.
    Includes index.
    Summary: Provides step-by-step instructions for forty-one card tricks, in such categories as "Prediction," "Gambling," and "Mind Reading."
    ISBN 0-8069-8232-2
    1. Card tricks—Juvenile literature. [1. Card tricks. 2. Magic tricks.] I. Title.
GV1549.L53   1990
795.4'38—dc20   90-46641
                                                 CIP
                                                 AC

10 9 8 7 6 5 4 3 2 1

First paperback edition published in 1992 by
Sterling Publishing Company, Inc.
387 Park Avenue South, New York, N.Y. 10016
© 1991 by Bob Longe
Distributed in Canada by Sterling Publishing
% Canadian Manda Group, P.O. Box 920, Station U
Toronto, Ontario, Canada M8Z 5P9
Distributed in Great Britain and Europe by Cassell PLC
Villiers House, 41/47 Strand, London WC2N 5JE, England
Distributed in Australia by Capricorn Link Ltd.
P.O. Box 665, Lane Cove, NSW 2066
Manufactured in the United States of America
All rights reserved

Sterling ISBN 0-8069-8232-2 Trade
        ISBN 0-8069-8233-0 Paper

Contents

Odds and Ends

Introduction

It has been more than forty years since the publication of my first book of card tricks. Over the years, I have come up with many card trick ideas—some based on old principles and some which I think are completely new. Why write a card trick book after all these years? I wrote it because it was needed. This is the book that no one else could write. It's the one I wish someone had put in my hands when I decided to start doing card tricks.

I have taught dozens of people of all ages how to do card tricks. When you do this, you realize that you don't want to teach *all* the card tricks, just the best; you don't want to teach *all* the moves, just the most useful. That's what this book comprises: the world's best tricks and some easy, useful "sleights." A sleight is a move that deceives the spectator. Sleights require a certain amount of manual dexterity. Some easy sleights are described in the first section of this book, *Nothing Up My Sleeve*, beginning on page 15.

There is no such thing as an old joke; if you haven't heard it before, it's new. So in this book you will find many "new" tricks that have been around for quite a while. They have been dusted off and shined up, however. Others are quite new. Several (mostly of my origination) have never before appeared in print. Still others originally appeared in my early booklets. For most readers, these tricks will be brand-new.

This is not an exhaustive collection of card tricks. For inclusion, a trick had to appeal to me *and* to spectators. I do perform all of these tricks. I included no tricks that were too dumb for me to do but would be perfect for you.

I describe *exactly* how I perform each trick. I provide the easiest way I can imagine. I have added an original wrinkle, if not an entire fold, to most tricks. I consider these tricks (immodestly, in some instances) the best impromptu card tricks ever invented.

How does anyone make up a card trick? First, I figure out an effect. Then I toy with a deck until a solution occurs to me. Often it takes months—sometimes years. And along the way, serendipity sometimes operates, and something new and wonderful pops up. For example, I have sought for years a simple way to have a chosen card appear at the point in the deck at which a spectator orders the performer to stop dealing. About a year ago, as I was toying with another effect altogether, the solution occurred to me. The trick appears in this book under the title *Ups and Downs*, on page 58.

I have mentioned *effect*. In card magic, as in other branches of magic, the effect is everything. Unfortunately, many otherwise proficient magicians forget this. Hang around a magic shop awhile. You will see card experts trying desperately to fool one another. All you need is one good, *simple* way to do the trick, something that will impress spectators, not magicians. Even if magicians *are* impressed, they will pretend they aren't.

It doesn't matter how you accomplish the effect, or how slick you are—all that matters is the effect itself.

On the other hand, I am prejudiced against tricks done with setups, trick cards, two decks, or any kind of apparatus. Somebody hands you a deck; you do an astonishing trick. That's magic. If the deck cannot be examined, even the dumbest spectator will realize that he can buy the same trick at the old magic store.

Compared to most card performers, I am not particularly proficient with sleights. I doubt that I could fool many magicians, except perhaps with a new principle. But I fool virtually all laymen. The reason: With the equipment I have (including small hands, by the way) I do excellent card tricks. You can too, starting now.

Getting Started

The vast majority of tricks in this book requires no sleight of hand, i.e., no manipulative ability. You must be able to shuffle a deck, but that's about it.

But the idea of "no sleights" should not be interpreted to mean "no skill." Every trick, whether it calls for prestidigitation or not, requires considerable skill. What skill? The skill of *presenting a trick properly*. I have seen performers with amazing technical ability who never amaze, nor do they entertain or amuse. Worst of all, they never perform *magic*. They do astonish with their flourishes, in the same way a juggler astonishes. We want to astonish, all right, but we also want to do magic, to create an atmosphere of mystery and romance. It takes skill.

The first section of the book, *Nothing Up My Sleeve*, introduces six easy sleights used in several of the tricks. Included here are three easy methods of forcing a card, a false cut, and two other simple, undetectable sleights.

Most of the tricks are presented in the second section of the book, *The Great Card Tricks*. Included are five mind-reading tricks in which the performer can demonstrate telepathic powers.

In the third section of the book, *Odds and Ends*, you will find *Whoops!*, which explains what to do when something goes wrong. And no matter how careful you are, once in a while something will.

It is not enough merely to "know" a trick. Even the simplest trick requires the four Ps: *preparation*, thorough *practice*, convincing *patter*, and smooth *presentation*.

Preparation: Read over the trick, going through every aspect with a deck of cards. Run through it a few times to make sure you understand the basic principle. Now *think* about it. No two persons are going to do a trick exactly the same way. See if you can develop a unique angle or a simplification that will particularly suit you.

There is nothing absolutely binding about anyone's instructions, including mine. Understand, however, that in this book the method given is tried and true; the trick has been done hundreds of times to good effect using the exact method described.

Practice: Work out every move precisely. You must be *smooth*.

Patter: Here is where mystery, romance, and magic come in. Spectators *want* to be amazed; give them an excuse, a reason. Make strength of weakness. Why must they count the cards? You want to be scrupulously fair. Why are you removing a card from the top? It's your lucky card, and the spectator must tap the deck with it. It doesn't matter how preposterous the story is. Often as not, the more ridiculous the story, the more entertaining the trick.

Do *not* narrate, "Now I deal three cards, and now I place them over here." No spectator likes being treated like an idiot. Obviously, you must sometimes explain what you are doing and why you are doing it, but do not make this your standard procedure.

Develop the kind of patter appropriate to your personality. If you are bombastic, develop lively, high-tension patter. If you are reserved, present reasoned experiments. Don't try to be something you aren't. In other words, don't don the magician's cape, becoming the all-knowing, the all-powerful. Just be yourself. Knowing a few card tricks does not make you superior. And if you are, in fact, superior, try to keep this fact concealed. In other words, try not to be obnoxious. Many magicians neglect this step.

Presentation: Take care of the first three Ps, and you won't have to worry about the fourth P, *presentation*. There are two rules: Never do a trick twice, and quit while you're ahead.

Some tricks are designed to be repeated—the mystery is enhanced with repetition—but most should be done only once. A repetition could lead to discovery.

Occasionally spectators will insist that you do a trick again. Perhaps they will say, "You're afraid we'll catch on." This is quite true, of course. But you respond, "Not at all. A repetition would bore you. It would certainly bore me. I have many other wonders to show you."

When asked to perform, you will be tempted to do at least a dozen tricks. Three or four are plenty. If your audience begs for more, you can always accommodate them.

I explain the tricks in considerable detail, perhaps more than you need or want. One reason is that I have always resented it when a card-book author left out important details. Another reason is that it is not enough for you to know just the basic trick; it's important that you learn *exactly* what I do. Often enough, the real secret of a successful trick is something which may, to the casual reader, seem insignificant: a word, a gesture, pacing, whatever.

I recommend, then, that you try each trick in much the same way as it is presented here. Inevitably, you will come to perform it your own way.

You have heard of "self-working" tricks. There is no such thing. *All* tricks—from those requiring several sleights to those requiring none—must be worked skilfully by the performer.

Tips

You are about to learn lessons I paid for with failure, chagrin, and self-recrimination.

1. When a card is selected, have it shown to other spectators. Yes, it's true—sometimes a spectator will lie.

2. No matter how ardently you are importuned, do not reveal how a trick is done. This applies to even the simplest trick. When you give a trick away, you spoil it for the spectators, and you ruin your reputation as "Mr. Magic." The spectators can no longer enjoy the mystery and the romance, and instead of a magician, you have become someone who bought a book the spectators did not buy. You will be delighted to follow this advice once you have explained a trick and have heard a spectator say, "Oh, is that all?"

Spectators *want* to believe in magic. Years ago, I violated this principle. A lady I knew fairly well told me that she had seen a marvellous trick the night before. A friend of the family had placed an empty beer bottle on the kitchen table, had wrapped it in paper, and had then squashed the paper. The bottle had disappeared!

I reluctantly gave in to her entreaties to explain the trick. "He was sitting at the table, right? The paper he wrapped the bottle in had to be stiff enough to hold the shape. As he talked, he brought the wrapped bottle over the edge of the table and let the bottle drop in his lap."

"But that isn't what he did," my friend insisted.

"No problem," I said. "Then it was magic."

Since then, I have *never* explained a trick.

3. *Never* let a spectator do a trick. If pressed, tell the spectator he can perform when you are done. If he insists, you *are* done. Give him the deck and walk away.

Sometimes I explain, "I don't think I could survive seeing for the 500th time someone dealing out three rows of cards with seven cards in each row."

Quite often, disappointment marks the face of the aspiring performer. "Oh, do you know that one?" he asks ruefully.

4. A card is selected, and you find it. No matter how many different ways you find the card, you are still doing only one trick. You can do this several times, and it might be entertaining. But throw in some variety. Very few of the tricks in this book begin with "Take a card," so you have a nice variety to choose from. Mix up your tricks. The more diversity you display, the more entertained the spectators will be, and the more impressed they will be with your ability.

5. If you are fascinated with performing card tricks, you will undoubtedly consult many other books of legerdemain. Just remember this: It's not enough that a trick may be easy to do; it must also be *worth* doing.

NOTHING UP MY SLEEVE

The Peek

Magicians use *The Peek* to sneak a look at a card without being observed. There are many methods, most of them requiring some sleight of hand.

The Peek is often called *The Glimpse.* I prefer the former term—it sounds sneakier.

The methods I present here are actually *Peek* substitutes, but that does not matter. You need to know the name of a particular card in the deck—the top, the bottom, or the second from the bottom—but you do not wish to unduly arouse the suspicions of your audience.

Suppose you wish to learn the name of the top card. Choose from these four methods.

1. Peek at the bottom card while toying with the deck and chatting with the spectators. Give the cards an overhand shuffle, drawing off the last few cards individually so that the bottom card ends up on top.

2. Look at it ahead of time.

3. Fan through the deck, saying, "I want to get a mental picture of all the cards," or (even more preposterously), "I want to make sure all the cards are here." Note the top card.

4. Fan through the cards, saying, "I want to remove my bad luck card. Otherwise this might not work." Fan through once, noting the top card. Then

find the queen of spades, or some other "bad luck card," and toss it aside. This method is particularly effective.

There are many other methods of sighting a card. If you investigate card-trick literature, you will come across at least a half-dozen.

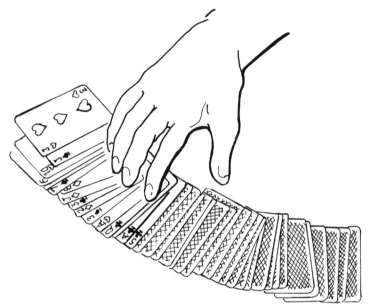

Illus. 1.   One means of forcing the top card in a deck. As you hold the deck, have a spectator cut off a portion of the cards, and then have him place them face up on the rest of the deck. Turn the deck over and spread the cards out on the table.

Forces

A *force* is a method of getting a spectator to select the card that you want him to. There are many methods, most requiring some sleight of hand. The three offered here are quite convincing and easy to do.

One-Cut Force

You must know the top card. See *The Peek* (page 17). As you hold the deck, have a spectator cut off a portion of cards and turn them face up on the rest of the deck.

Immediately turn the deck over and spread the cards out on the table (Illus. 1). Push through the face-up cards to the first face-down card. Point to it, saying, "Please take a look at the card." It is, of course, the original top card which you sighted.

There is a temptation to say, "Look at the card you cut to." As with the trick *Crisscross*, I think it's a mistake to be that specific. I don't want the spectator to be thinking, "Hmm. *Is* that the card I cut to?"

The Face-Up Force

This is a quick, deceptive force, which I occasionally use to discover a chosen card. You must know the top card. Have a spectator take a card from the deck, turn it face up, and place it on top. He then cuts a pile from the top and sets it on the table. You turn the remaining cards in your hand face up and place them beside the cutoff portion, Take the cutoff portion (with the face-up card on top), turn it face up, and place it on top of the other pile.

Pick up the deck and turn it face down. Hand it to the spectator and ask him to look through to the face-up card and look at the randomly selected card below it.

You may prefer to fan through yourself, chatting about freedom of choice in cutting the cards. Separate the cards below the face-up card and offer the next card (originally the top card, of course) for him to look at.

Actually, all that has happened is that a face-up card was placed upon the force card and the cards were cut. The handling, however, obscures this and convinces the spectator that he has freely chosen the card. Practise this one a bit before trying it in public; smoothness is the key.

Double-Turnover Force

Again you must know the top card. See *The Peek* (page 17). As you hold the deck, ask a spectator to cut off a small packet and turn it face up on the deck. Then have him cut off a larger packet and turn it face up on the deck. Fan through the face up cards to the first face-down card. Extend the face-down pile to the spectator, asking him to look at his card. It is the original top card.

The False Cut _____

In the grand scheme of things—even in the little scheme of card magic—a false cut is probably not terribly important. You can perform just about any trick without it. Still, it's a handy way to confuse the spectators as to how the cards are positioned. And it provides a fillip, a little flourish that puts the icing on the cake.

I like to use this particular false cut. Many others seem too simple or too fancy—and some are too difficult.

The One-Finger Cut

This is unique among false cuts, in that the phony one looks more genuine than the real one.

First, the *real* cut. The deck is held from above in the right hand near the right edge, second finger at the front, thumb at the back, and first finger either curled or slightly bent. The left hand, fingers up, approaches the deck from the rear (Illus. 2).

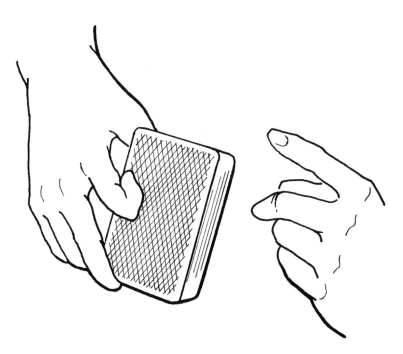

Illus. 2.   The first step of a "true" cut.

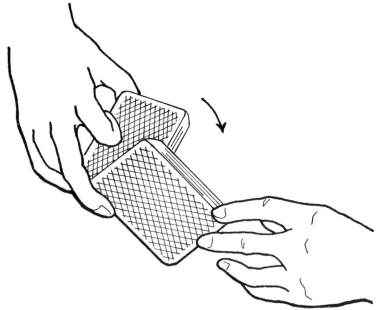

Illus. 3. Pivot the top half of the deck, revolving the cards around the second finger of your right hand.

The first finger of the left hand does the work. With the tip, it pivots the top half of the deck, revolving the cards around the second finger of the right hand (Illus. 3). The left hand moves directly in front of the right hand so that the top half of the deck drops into the left hand (Illus. 4).

To complete the legitimate cut, the right hand places its half on top of the cards in the left hand.

Here is the *false* cut. After you pivot the top half into the left hand, bring the cards in the right hand directly over the top of the portion in the left hand and set them on the table. The right hand returns, takes the pile from the left hand, which has remained stationary, and places the pile on top of the cards on the table.

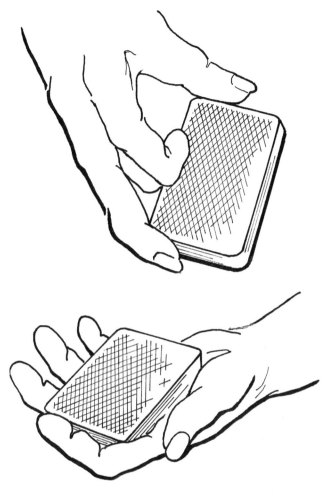

Illus. 4. The top half of the deck drops into your left hand.

There are two keys: bringing the pile in your right hand *directly over* the cards in your left hand as you set the pile on the table, and keeping your left hand stationary when you return with your right hand to get the other half. The cut takes just a few seconds and is totally deceptive.

The Glide

Used properly—which is to say, sparingly—this is one of the most useful moves in card magic. You show the bottom card of the deck and, presumably, place it on the table. Only it is not the same card. You actually deal out the second card from the bottom.

The maneuver, of course, should never be used as a trick by itself. Even the dullest spectator will have an inkling as to what actually happened.

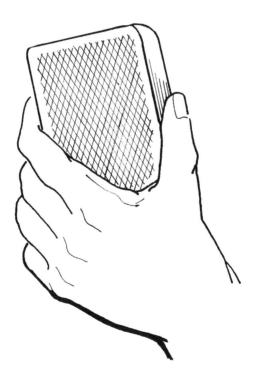

Illus. 5.   Hold the deck in your left hand, at the sides, and from above.

The deck is held in the left hand at the sides from above (Illus. 5). The cards are lifted, showing the bottom card to the spectators (Illus. 6). Note that the hand is gripping nearer the back of the deck than the front, and that the second and third fingers extend over the side of the deck past the first joint. The reason will become apparent.

The deck is tilted down again, and the second and third fingers bend under and draw the bottom card back one-half inch or so. Illus. 7 shows the view from underneath. The second card from the bottom is now drawn out with the second and third

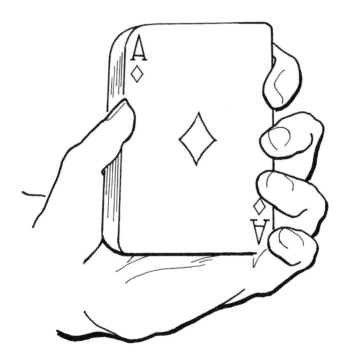

Illus. 6.   Lift the cards and show the bottom card to the spectators.

fingers of the right hand. When the card is drawn out about an inch, the right thumb takes it at the top so that the card is gripped beneath by the second and third fingers and at the top by the thumb. The card is placed face down on the table.

Illus. 7.   Draw the bottom card back one-half inch. This view is from underneath.

THE GREAT
CARD TRICKS

Prediction _____

Presto Prediction

This trick appeared almost forty years ago in a booklet I published. The trick was recently credited to someone else. I don't invent so many good tricks that I can afford to let that pass: I invented it, and besides, my version is better.

Few tricks have a climax as startling as this one. The principle is just about impossible to detect, but what really makes the trick work is the patter, the romance. I have always felt that a weakness can be turned into a strength if you only give the problem enough thought. In this instance, the spectators are dealing cards, selecting, counting down. In other words, this has all the earmarks of a "mathematical" trick, a no-brainer, a trick anyone could do. Indeed it is. But the patter makes it all seem logical, if not absolutely necessary. So at the climax of the trick, be sure to try the suggested patter.

Hand the deck to a spectator for shuffling, saying, "Now I am going to attempt to predict the future. The odds are fifty-two to one against my doing this, but I think it's going to work this time. You see, I've missed the last sixty-three times, so I'm way overdue."

Take the deck back, holding it with your fingertips, so that all can see that you are doing nothing tricky. "Watch carefully. I want you to see that I do not change the position of a single card. I'm going to fan through the deck and remove a prediction card."

Demonstrate by fanning through the cards, faces towards you, noting the value of the top card. Close up the cards. Let us suppose that the top card is an eight.

"Watch carefully now!" With the cards facing you, again fan through them, starting at the bottom. Since you noted an eight on top, count to eight from the bottom and note the card at that position. Let us say it is the five of diamonds. Continue fanning until you come to the corresponding card in color and value—in this instance, the five of hearts. Meticulously lift the five of hearts from the deck and place it face down on the table, stating, "This is my prediction card." While doing all this, handle the cards openly to emphasize that you are doing *nothing tricky* with the deck.

Hand the deck to a second spectator. "Please turn the deck face up and deal the cards one at a time into a pile." Once he deals past the card you noted, casually say, "You can stop whenever you want." When he does stop, tell him he may deal a few more, take a few back, whatever he wishes.

Take the undealt cards from the spectator and place them face down. Turn the dealt cards face down. The position now is as follows: The top card of the undealt pile indicates the number down in the dealt pile at which the match for your prediction card lies. In our example, the top card of one pile is an eight, and the eighth card down in the other pile is the five of diamonds, which corresponds to your prediction card, the five of hearts.

Point out the two face-down piles to a third spectator. "Perhaps you have seen demonstrations where the performer asks you to choose a pile and then he takes whatever pile he wants. In this case, I want you to pick up a pile. That will be the pile that you will actually use."

Sound convincing? Of course. But, as you will see, it doesn't matter which pile he picks up. Suppose he takes the pile with the eight on top. You say, "What we are going to do is turn over the top card of your pile—not yet—and count down that number in this pile." Pick up the other pile and continue, "An ace has a value of one, a jack eleven, a queen twelve, and a king thirteen." This statement is particularly effective when the card is *not* one of these, for it creates the impression that you have no idea of what the card is.

The third spectator turns over the top card of his pile; you slowly count off the cards from your pile, setting aside the card arrived at. In our example, the spectator turned over an eight, so you count off eight cards, setting aside the eighth one, the five of diamonds.

Suppose that when you offer the choice of piles the third spectator picks up the pile containing the card that matches your prediction card. Simply say, "Now I will turn over the top card of my pile, and we will count down that number in the pile you have chosen." Be sure to mention the business about the value of ace, jack, queen, and king. Let the spectator count off the cards, and you take the final card of the count and place it face down on the table.

You now have two face-down cards on the table: your prediction card and the card "chosen" by the spectators. Gather up the rest of the deck, leaving the two face-down cards.

What you say now triples the trick's effectiveness. "Let's review. First, the deck was thoroughly shuffled. Without changing the position of a single card, I removed the prediction card. Then you (the second spectator) dealt off as many cards as you wanted, stopped whenever you wanted. Finally, you (the third spectator) chose a pile, and we actually used the pile you chose. In other words, we tried to arrive at the choice of a card completely by chance. Why did we go through all this? Because if I offered you the choice of a card, you might think I had some way of forcing my selection on you. Instead, we have guaranteed that a card was chosen at random."

Set aside the deck. Take the two cards at the outer edge. "If I have correctly predicted the future, these two cards should match each other in color—and in value." Face the two cards simultaneously. When you gather the cards up after enjoying their astonishment, it's fun to add, "I feel sorry for the next fifty-one people I do this for."

Note: Occasionally, when fanning through the cards for your prediction card, you will see that it is among those that will be counted off. Obviously, the trick will not work. Shake your head, close up the cards, and hand them to a spectator, saying, "Please shuffle them again. I can't seem to picture a card; the vibrations just aren't right. Perhaps another shuffle will help."

Colorful Prediction

With this trick, by using an unprepared deck, you apparently correctly estimate the number of red and black cards in two piles.

For this one, you need a complete deck of fifty-two cards. Let a spectator shuffle the deck. Take it back and begin dealing into a face-down pile. After you have dealt fifteen or more, invite the spectator to tell you to stop whenever he wishes.

As you deal, count the cards. Try to keep your lips from moving. When he says stop, give him the dealt pile. Ask him his favorite color, red or black. Suppose he says red, and further suppose that his pile contains twenty-three cards. You say, "Bad luck. I have three more red cards than you have black."

Repeat the assertion. Now deal your cards face up, counting the red cards aloud as you go. The spectator deals his cards face up, counting the blacks. Sure enough, you have three more reds than he has blacks.

Why?

To understand, take a deck of cards, shuffle it, and deal it into two piles of twenty-six cards each. Suppose you have nineteen black cards in one pile. You must also have seven red cards in that pile. This means that the other pile must contain nineteen red cards and seven black cards. So, no matter how you shuffle, when you have two piles of twenty-six cards, you will always have the same number of black cards in one pile as you have red cards in the other.

This will be clearer if we take an extreme example or two. If you have twenty-six black cards in one pile, you will have twenty-six red cards in the other. You could say, "I have the same number of reds in my pile as you have blacks in yours."

It would work the same if you had twenty-five red cards and one black in your pile. The spectator would have twenty-five blacks and one red. And you, naturally, would have the same number of red cards as he has blacks.

If you tried to pass that off as a trick, however, very few spectators would be deceived, particularly if you do repeats. Therefore, you disguise the principle by working with unequal piles and performing a simple calculation.

When you performed the trick as above, the spectator had twenty-three cards. That's three less than twenty-six. You, therefore, have three more than twenty-six. This means that you have three more red cards than he has black. For that matter, you have three more black cards than he has red.

Back to the trick. The spectator is astonished at your clairvoyance, but you have only just begun. Have the spectator shuffle his packet of twenty-three, and you shuffle your packet. You may even exchange packets and shuffle. Then you take your original packet and begin dealing onto his, asking him again to tell you when to stop. Once more you keep track of the number.

He had twenty-three, so you begin counting with twenty-four. When he tells you to stop, you again know the number of cards he has in his pile.

"Which do you want this time, red or black?" Suppose he chooses black, and that he now has thirty cards in his pile.

"Good selection. You now hold four more blacks than I have reds."

In other words, he has four more cards than twenty-six.

You may repeat the trick a number of times, remembering to deal from the larger packet to the smaller. In our example, the piles would be shuffled again, and you would make sure to deal from the pile of thirty onto the other, which, of course, contains twenty-two.

The trick, like many good ones, is a combination of a hidden principle and verbal chicanery. You can throw spectators off further by stating your prediction in different ways.

There are four ways you could state the preceding prediction:

1. You now hold four more blacks than I have reds.

2. You now have four more reds than I have blacks.

3. I now have four fewer blacks than you have reds.

4. I now have four fewer reds than you have blacks.

Three-Card Surprise

When I invented this trick, I discovered that it is doubly astonishing. It is absolutely baffling and entertaining to spectators. And it is astonishing to me that it should be so well received. I consider it among the best tricks I perform.

The original version of this trick must be as old as card tricks. Long ago I came across a good version. Unfortunately, two decks were required (an automatic turn-off for me), and the move required at the end seemed contrived, unnecessary, and unsatisfactory. Recently I solved the problem of the ending, and in the process came up with what amounts to a new trick—with one deck.

Because the effect is similar to that of *Presto Prediction*, you should probably not do these two in the same set. The effect is that you correctly predict three cards chosen by a spectator or spectators.

Have the deck shuffled. Take the cards back and fan through them, faces towards you, saying, "We are going to take turns selecting cards. First I'll select one, and then you'll select one."

As you spread the cards, note the top card. Remove a card from the deck of the same value and color. If the top card is the six of diamonds, for instance, you remove the six of hearts. Without showing it to the spectators, place it face down on the table. Spread the rest of the cards face down on the table, inviting a spectator to choose one and place it face up on your card. It is important that you make no mention of telling the future or matching cards; you two are simply taking turns selecting cards.

Tell the spectator, "A very good choice. Now I'll select another one." Fan through the cards as before, and remove the card that is the same color and value as the one which he just placed face up. As you do so, mutter about how this must be the world's most tedious card experiment. Place the card face down to the right of your first choice. Set the deck down and say, "You will choose each card in a different way. This time, I would like you to cut a pile off the deck."

When he cuts the cards, take the one he cut to and place it face up on top of your second choice.

Make sure you replace the cutoff pile on top so that the card you originally sighted remains on top.

Compliment the spectator on his selection and fan through the cards once more, muttering about how boring this experiment is. This time remove a card of the same color and value as the spectator's second selection and place the card face down to the right of the other two.

"Now we'll try yet another way of selecting a card," you say. Retaining the deck in your hand, tell the spectator, "Cut off a small packet, turn it face up, and place it on top of the deck." After he does so, say, "Now cut off a larger packet, turn it face up, and place it on top of the deck." This is *Double-Turnover Force* (page 20).

Explain, "Now we'll go to the card you cut to." Fan through the face-up cards and take out the first face-down card. It, of course, is the original top card, the one you sighted at the beginning of the trick. Place the card face up on top of your third face-down card.

It is important that you more or less follow the patter I have given. You don't want to put the spectators on guard by mentioning things like prediction or coincidence or any of the usual baloney.

Set the rest of the deck aside, saying, "I know exactly what you're thinking. Are there extra cards on the table? Did he slip in an extra card or two?"

Place the third set of two, the one on your right, on top of the middle set. Then place the set on the left on top of all. Now the top card matches the bottom card, and the other two pairs match each other face-to-face. I have inserted a little sneakiness into the routine here. "I can assure you that there are exactly six cards here."

Pick up the packet of six and hold it in the dealing position in the left hand. Take off the top card in your right hand with your right thumb, counting out, "One." Take off the second card in the same way, dealing it on top of the first in your right hand. You count, "Two."

Continue through the fifth card, counting aloud for each one. For the sixth card, you pause ever so slightly, saying, "And six." And place the sixth card on the bottom.

Instantly, take off the top two cards and drop them on the table. Next to them drop the next two cards. And next to them drop the last set of two. While doing this, say, "Six cards. Three sets of two."

The business of counting the cards and dropping them on the table in pairs has taken some time to explain. But the execution must be done snappily.

After a brief pause, turn over the face-down card in each pair, showing that the pairs match up in color and value. At this point it is frivolous to say anything; the climax speaks for itself. You will be delighted to hear such comments as, "But how could you know that I would pick that?"

Transposition _____

Tick Tock Trick

To my delight, this trick of mine appeared in the September, 1949 issue of *Conjurors' Magazine*. This trick is always received well, and it is a nice change of pace from more conventional effects.

You deal twelve cards in a face-up circle, each card indicating an hour on the clock. Start with one o'clock and deal around to twelve o'clock, calling off each number (or time) as you deal. The card at twelve o'clock should be pushed a little above the circle so that the spectators will have no trouble telling what card lies at what time. The queen of spades is placed in the middle and is dubbed "the card of mystery." A spectator mentally selects one of the cards and remembers the time at which it lies.

Turn your back and tell the spectator to quietly count from the deck a number of cards equal to the hour at which his selected card lies. If his card lies at five o'clock, he counts off five cards. These cards are placed in the spectator's pocket, or are otherwise concealed.

Now gather up the cards, apparently casually. Chat with the spectators as you do so. Pick up "the card of mystery" first and place it face up in your left hand. Pick up the rest of the cards in reverse order, starting with the card at twelve o'clock. The last one placed face up in your left hand is the card at one o'clock. Put these cards face down on top of the deck.

Now would be a good time to perform the *One-Finger Cut*, on page 21.

Have the spectator take the cards he has concealed and place them on top of the deck while you look away. You must now get rid of the top card. Riffle the end of the deck a few times, and then say, "No, I didn't do anything." Take off the top card and show it. "See? It's not *your* card, and it's not the card of mystery." Place the card in the middle of the deck. To throw a little dust in their eyes, take the bottom card also, show it, and place it in the middle of the deck.

Deal the cards face down into a circle, starting with one o'clock. The thirteenth card is placed in the middle, and you refer to it as "the card of mystery."

Ask the spectator what time he selected. The card at that time is turned over; it is "the card of mystery." And the card in the center? Ask the spectator to name his card. Turn over the center card, saying, "Ah, your card is the new card of mystery."

Easy Aces

Every card trickster knows at least one four-ace trick, and most know several. Card performers love to do false shuffles, multiple palms, and top changes as they magically collect the aces into one pile. This version magically collects the aces into one pile, and requires no sleights.

When you hear how this one is done, you may decide that it's a little too gutsy for you. "Aw, shucks! Everyone will see how it's done." *No one* will see how it's done. The dirty work is done before anyone expects it, and with excellent misdirection.

Take the four aces from the pack, show them, and place them in a face-down row on the table. On top of each ace deal three cards face down. Set aside the rest of the deck. Place the piles one on top of the other, forming one pile.

"Obviously," you explain, "every fourth card is an ace." Fan the cards before the spectators, showing that this is true. As you fan through, say, "Three cards and an ace, three cards and an ace, three cards and an ace, and three cards and an ace." Even up the cards slowly and meticulously, demonstrating that you are performing no sleights.

From the top of the packet, deal four cards in a row on the table, saying, "Here we have one, two, three, ace." Casually take the top card of the packet in your hand. "So what's this card?" you ask, tapping the ace with the card in your hand.

The spectator will probably say that it is an ace. Regardless, you say, "Turn it over, please."

As he does so, *casually place the card in your hand on the bottom of the packet.* All attention, of course, is on the card being turned over.

Turn the ace face down. Deal a row of cards on top of the cards you just dealt, saying, "One, two, three, ace." Finish dealing the rest of the packet in the same manner, repeating, "One, two, three, ace."

The spectators are convinced that the four aces are in the fourth pile. Actually, the bottom card of the fourth pile is an ace, and the rest of the pile consists of ordinary cards. The bottom one of the third pile is an ordinary card, while the other three in that pile are aces.

Pick up piles one and two, and drop them on the deck. Take the ace from the bottom of the original fourth pile and place it face up in front of that pile.

Take the ordinary card from the bottom of the original third pile and place it face up in front of that pile.

"One pile of aces," you say, "and one pile of ordinary cards." Then, suiting action to words, you add, "All we have to do is exchange the markers, snap the fingers, and the cards magically change places."

Turn over the three ordinary cards first, saying, "Now *these* are the ordinary cards." Turn over the aces, as you say, "And *these* are the aces."

Tricky Transpo

This trick is the easiest transposition trick ever—it is also a baffler. A word of warning, however. The participating spectators are required to remember both a card and a number. Do not perform this one as a part of your regular routine; save it for times when you have bright, cooperative spectators.

Ask for the assistance of two spectators. Give the deck to the first spectator and then turn your back. Give these directions to the first spectator: "Please shuffle the cards. Now think of an even number, preferably one under twenty. Quietly count off that number of cards. When you are done, hand the deck to my other assistant."

Direct the second spectator as follows: "Will you shuffle the deck, please? Now think of an odd number, preferably one under twenty. Quietly count off that number of cards."

When the second spectator is done, continue: "Please set the rest of the deck aside; we won't be using it anymore. Now put both piles together, and I would like one of you to shuffle the new pile. Now, without changing the position of any card, I want both of you to see what card lies at the number you thought of. I would like each of you to remember your card and the number you thought of."

Turn back to the spectators and take the pile of cards. Place them behind your back, saying, "I am going to attempt to transpose the two selected cards."

When you put the cards behind your back, take the bottom card in your right hand and, starting with the top card, *quietly* deal the rest of the cards on top of it, reversing their order. While doing this, make small talk about the tremendous miracle you are attempting to perform. Bring the cards forward. Ask the first spectator for his even number. He tells you and, without changing the position of any cards (taking them one *under* the other), count down to that number. Ask the second spectator to name his card. Show that his card now lies at that number.

Replace the card in the exact same spot in the pile, and replace the cards on top so that they are in precisely the same order. Ask the second spectator what his number was. Count down to that number in the same way as you did previously. Before showing the card at that number, ask the first spectator to name his card. Show that it is now at that number.

The trick is a little complex, but I love it. I'm still not dead sure why it works, so every time I perform it, I am at least as astonished as the spectators.

Estimation _____

Easy Estimation

Tricks don't get much better than this one. Apparently you can gauge the precise number of cards a spectator cuts.

Have the deck shuffled and set down. Tell a spectator to cut off a packet of cards, not too large. Then you cut off a packet, making sure it contains several more cards than the spectator's pile. Turn your back, saying, "We'll each count our cards. Then I'll tell you exactly how many you have."

With your back turned to the spectator, count your cards as he counts his. Suppose you have twenty-two. Can you make a trick out of telling the spectator that you have twenty-two cards? It doesn't seem likely, does it? Yet that is, in effect, exactly what you do.

When you turn back to the spectator, say, "I have the same number you have, three left over, and enough more to make your pile total nineteen." Repeat the statement to make sure it sinks in.

"Now let's count our cards together." As he counts his cards into a pile, you simultaneously count yours into a separate pile. The cards should be counted deliberately, and you should count out loud.

Let us suppose he had thirteen cards. You stop dealing at the same time as he does. "Thirteen," you say. "The same number you have. And I said, three left over." Deal three cards from your pile to one side, counting aloud. "Three left over. And I said that I had enough left over to make your pile total nineteen." Point to his pile. "You have thirteen." *Count now on his pile.* "Fourteen, fifteen, sixteen, seventeen, eighteen, nineteen." You were exactly right.

So far as I know, this is the only trick based *solely* on the use of words. As I indicated, what you *really* said to the spectator was, "I counted my cards, and it turned out I had twenty-two."

Let's try another form: "I have the same number you have and enough more to make a total of twenty-two." Wouldn't fool many people, would it?

Try this: "I have twenty-two cards, but I decided to subtract three from it, giving me nineteen."

Still not tricky enough? Here's the actual form again: "I have the same number you have, three left over, and enough more to make your pile total nineteen."

You could also say, "I have the same number you have, two left over, and enough more to make your pile total twenty."

What you do, of course, is subtract a small number—two, three, or four—from your total number of cards. In the example, you counted twenty-two cards. Supposing that, instead of three, you decide that four should be the number left over. You subtract four from twenty-two, giving you eighteen. You now have two critical numbers, and you say, "I have the same number you have, four left over, and enough more to make your pile total eighteen." Note that these statements will work when you have a pile containing several more cards than the spectator's.

The trick can be repeated with no danger of spectators discovering the secret. To throw them off the track, use different numbers—two, three, four—for the number of cards left over.

Let's make sure you have it. The spectator cuts off a packet. Make sure it's no more than twenty cards. Cut off a pile containing several more cards than his. Turn away, telling the spectator to count his cards while you count yours. Suppose you have twenty-five. You will choose a small number—two, three, or four—to subtract from it. Let's say you choose two. You subtract two from twenty-five, giving you twenty-three. When you turn back, you state, "I have the same number you have, two left over, and enough more to make your pile total twenty-three." Then complete the trick as described above.

There are two things that throw the spectators off: the few extra cards that you count off, and the completion of the count, not on your pile, *but on the spectator's pile.*

Digital Estimation

Here's one I made up many, many years ago. I have had considerable fun with it ever since. It's a pretty good follow-up to *Easy Estimation.*

You need a complete fifty-two-card deck. Two spectators each cut off a pile and are asked to hold the packets flat in their palms. You say, "I am going to estimate the number of cards each of you is holding and break the result down to its lowest digit. Then I will find a card to verify my estimation."

The effectiveness of this trick depends on your ability to playact. As you do the following, pause from time to time and study the piles the spectators are holding, creating the impression that you are performing a difficult feat of judgment.

What you actually do is run the remaining cards from hand to hand, faces toward you, apparently seeking an appropriate estimation card, but actually counting them. You will find you can do the counting rapidly and easily if you run the cards in groups of three. Don't forget to pause in your counting here and there to gauge the spectators' piles.

When you get the total, reduce it to a digit. Suppose the total is twenty-three; add the two and three together, giving you five. With a total of twenty-nine, add the two and nine, giving you eleven; then you add one and one, giving you a final digit of two.

Subtract your digit from either seven or sixteen, whichever gives you a single digit. Continuing to fan through the cards, find a card of that value and place it face down on the table.

For example, if you count twenty-three cards, add the digits together, giving you five. Subtract five from seven, giving you two. Find a two among your cards and place it face down on the table.

Another example: You count twenty-five cards. Add the two digits and you get seven. You are to subtract from either seven or sixteen. Since subtracting it from seven would give you zero, you subtract it from sixteen, giving you nine. Find a nine among your cards and place it face down on the table.

Now tell the spectators this: "I would like you each to count your cards carefully, and then mentally break your total down to one digit. For example, if you have fifteen cards, you would add the one and five together, giving you six."

When the spectators are done, have them each give their digit. Add these two together and break them down to a single figure. Turn over your estimation card and take a bow.

Why does it work? Let's start with a fifty-two-card deck. The digits five and two add up to seven. And no matter how you divide the fifty-two-card deck, the various piles when added together and broken down to a digit will produce seven.

So, when you count your pile, presumably looking for a card to signify your estimation, you can get the right answer by reducing your total to a digit and subtracting from seven, or from any two numbers that add up to seven, like sixteen, twenty-five, thirty-four, forty-three, or fifty-two, so long as you reduce your total to a single digit.

The trick can be repeated as above, but I prefer this: "To make it even more difficult, I will try to estimate the number of cards held by *three* spectators. Again, I will break down the total and select an estimation card."

Have three spectators cut off small packets and hold them flat on their palms. Scrutinize the packets. Then fan through the remaining cards, finding your estimation card by counting and subtracting from seven or sixteen, as before. The spectators count their piles, reduce the number in each pile to a digit, add the totals, and reduce that result to a digit. Naturally, your estimation is correct. Performing this twice works out about right. No use pushing your luck.

Note: Occasionally you cannot find the appropriate estimation card in your group of cards. Sometimes you can make do by removing two cards which add up to the appropriate number. Once in a blue moon, you might have to take out three cards. If it gets worse, just *tell* them the number before they count. Most of the time, however, you'll find one estimation card.

The Perfect Pile

Long ago, while working on the same principle used in *Digital Estimation*, I came up with the idea of making an estimation using a pile of cards. I removed from the deck a pile of cards to verify my estimation, not letting the spectators see the exact number, which was eight. Then I had two spectators divide the rest of the deck. Both counted their piles, reduced their number to a digit, added the digits together, and reduced the result to a digit. Naturally, the result was eight. Since the spectators had forty-four cards to divide (fifty-two minus eight), and four plus four is eight, they always ended up with eight.

So, the estimation always worked out. But the trick could not be repeated, at least not by the performer. But it certainly could be repeated by a spectator. If the spectator did exactly what the performer had done, he would duplicate the trick. So, over the years, I did not perform the trick very often. I have always liked the principle, however, and recently figured out a version that is a bit more mysterious and that will bear repeating.

Hand the deck to a spectator. "I would like you to shuffle those cards, and then cut off a pile and hand the rest of the deck to me."

After he does so, say, "I am going to try to make an exact estimation. But to make it more difficult for me, I want you to deal some cards into a separate pile, which we will not use. You can deal no cards, a few cards, or several cards."

Notice that you use the word "deal" instead of "count." You don't want the spectator to think in terms of counting the cards. The reason? While feigning indifference, you *are* counting the cards he deals aside.

So the spectator deals the card, cards, or no cards into a pile, and you have surreptitiously noted the number. The situation now is this: Some cards have been set aside, the spectator has a pile, and you have the rest of the deck.

Next comes some major-league baloney. Appraising the spectator's pile, you say, "This is most difficult. Not only must I estimate the number of cards, but also reduce that number to a digit."

Remove some cards from your pile, keeping the number secret from the spectators. You may hide them under your hand or stick them under a magazine—whatever. Hand the rest of your pile to a second spectator. Explain, "I have made my estimation and have placed a number of cards under my hand to confirm my choice."

As in *Digital Estimation*, have each spectator count his pile and reduce the number to a digit. Then the digits are added together and reduced to a single number.

Have one of the spectators count your estimation pile. It is the same number as the digit arrived at by the spectators. This is a good one to do at least one more time.

How do you know how many cards to take for your estimation pile? You can work it out for yourself if you're of a mind, but basically it depends on how many cards the spectator deals off and discards. You have two numbers to remember: sixteen and twenty-five. If the spectator deals off an even number, *you* use an even number—sixteen. If the spectator deals off an odd number, *you* use an odd number—twenty-five. Note that in both instances, you use a number whose digits add up to seven. In both cases, you subtract the number the spectator dealt off, and divide by two. This gives you the estimation number.

For example: The spectator deals off four cards. Since four is an even number, you will subtract it from sixteen. Four from sixteen is twelve. Half of twelve is six. So six is your estimation number, and you count off six cards as your estimation pile. Or, the spectator deals off seven cards. Seven is an odd number, so you subtract it from twenty-five. Seven from twenty-five is eighteen. Half of eighteen is nine. So there will be nine cards in your estimation pile. If your final number is in two digits, add the two together to get your estimation number.

Incidentally, with effects like these, the real trick is disguising the basic principle. So-called mathematical tricks should not appear to be so. After all, what credit accrues to the performer of a mathematical trick? He has not performed magic, but has presented a puzzle. The difference is this: With magic, you have a story.

The *Perfect Pile* trick could be presented as a puzzle. But it is far better to tell the story and act out the difficult estimation, pretending to gauge the number of cards held by the spectator. Of course it makes no sense. But it *is* magic.

Face-Up, Face-Down _____

Do-It-Yourself Discovery

This is one of the first impromptu card tricks I ever tried. The spectators' response told me that I had just performed real card magic. I was elated and determined to continue astonishing and mystifying.

The spectator shuffles the cards. Tell him to take half and give you the rest. "Now," you say, "while I turn my back, pick out a card, look at it, show it to the rest of the folks, and put it back on top of your pile."

Turn away and secretly turn two cards face up in your pile: the bottom card and the second card from the top.

When the spectator indicates that he is done, turn back, and tell the spectator to hold out his cards. Place your pile on top of his, even up the cards, and then direct him to place his arm behind his back, saying, "Now I want you to perform a little experiment with the cards behind your back."

Make sure of two things: that no spectator can see what goes on behind your assistant's back and that the assistant does not bring the cards forward until you are ready. To accomplish the latter, hover over the spectator, keeping alert to any premature disclosure. If he starts bringing the cards in front, say, "No, no, not until the completion of the experiment."

The position of the deck now: A card is face up second from the top, and a card is face up above the spectator's card in the middle of the deck.

"Take the top card . . . no, put that one on the bottom, so you'll know I'm not trying to fool you. Have you done that? All right. Take the *next* card, turn it face up, and stick it in the middle. Even up the cards."

Now you have the spectator bring the cards forward. Take the deck and fan through until you come to the face-up card. Ask the spectator to name his chosen card. Turn over the next card. "As you can see, you have located your chosen card yourself."

Once in a great while, the spectator will stick the card between your face-up card and the chosen card. You still have a decent trick. When you turn up the wrong card, simply say, "Oh, my! You missed by one." Turn up the next card, showing that it is the selected one. When doing tricks like this, where you are trying to hide the presence of face-up cards, it is best to use a deck with a white border.

Behind My Back

This trick is clever, snappy, and mystifying.

You deal cards into a pile. When you reach twelve, tell the spectator to tell you when to stop. Wherever he says stop, make sure you actually stop on an *even number*. Call no attention to the number, however.

Set the rest of the deck aside. Pick up your even number of cards and rapidly fan through in groups of three, silently counting off half of them. Turn these face up and shuffle the pile. The pile has the same number of cards face up as face down, but in no particular order. Don't explain. Simply hand the pile to a spectator, saying, "Face-up and face-down cards. Would you shuffle them even more."

Turn away and have the spectator place the cards in your hand after he finishes shuffling. Turning back towards the spectators, quickly count off half the cards from the top and turn the bottom half over. Bring the two piles forward, one in the right hand, the other in the left. Say, "You will find the same number of cards face up in each pile." Fan through each pile, counting the face-up cards aloud and showing that you are correct.

The trick's effectiveness is dependent upon how rapidly you can do the counting behind your back, so let me offer some hints. Suppose you have a pile of eighteen cards. When you take the cards from the spectator, you must count off nine. Holding the pile in your left hand, push them from the top one at a time into your right hand, taking them one *under* the other. As soon as you have nine in your right hand, bring that hand to the front. At the same time, turn your left hand so that it is *back side up* and bring that hand forward. The hands are brought forward virtually simultaneously.

It takes a while to describe, but the actual counting and production of the cards takes only a few seconds.

The Rare Reverse

Until you try this one, you will not believe what an astonishing effect it has on spectators.

Hand a spectator the deck and tell him, "I'd like you to help me with an experiment. Please shuffle the cards. Now deal four cards face down in a row." Take the deck back.

"While my back is turned, select one of the cards and show it around."

Turn away from the spectators. Turn the top card and the two bottom cards of the deck in your hand face up. Say to the spectator, "Now I would like you to gather up all four cards on the table and mix them up a little."

Turn, holding the deck in the left hand (Illus. 8). Casually wave the hand, showing the top and bottom cards, as you say, "Now comes the difficult part of the experiment, the part where magic comes in."

Take the four cards from the spectator in your right hand. Turn the left hand over, apparently showing the bottom card of the deck. Actually, of course, it is one face-up card.

Place the four cards face-to-face with the "bottom" card, saying, "First, we need to place these cards face up in the deck. Four cards, so we must turn the deck over four times."

You count, "One, two, three, four," as, with your right hand, you turn the deck over four times in

Illus. 8.   Holding the deck in your left hand, casually wave the deck, showing the top and the bottom cards.

your left hand. Turn them over by taking them at the outside edge and lifting, turning the deck towards you so that the former outside edge is now the end nearest your body (Illus. 9). The object is to confuse spectators as to which cards are face up and which are face down.

"Now—four magical shuffles." Give the cards four brief overhand shuffles.

"Magic time! What is the name of the card you thought of?"

When the spectator names his card, fan through the face-down cards quite deliberately, tossing out each face-up card as you come to it. Fan all the way

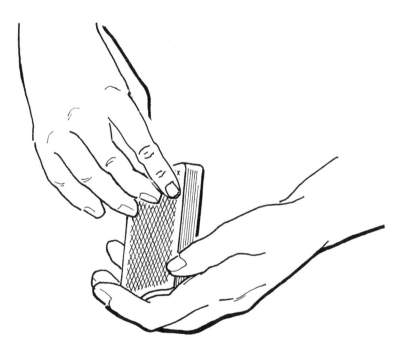

Illus. 9.   Take the deck at the outside edge and lift it, turning the deck towards you, so that the former outside edge is now the end nearest your body.

through the deck so spectators can see that there are only three face-up cards.

"The three *other* cards. And the card you thought of?" Turn the deck face up, fan through to the chosen card, and toss it out, saying, "It has magically turned itself over in the deck."

My Favorite Card

When you run through this trick on your own, you may decide it is just too dumb to fool anyone. Believe me, it is effective and deceptive. What's more, although it's over in fifteen or twenty seconds, it leaves a lasting impression.

Have a spectator shuffle the deck. Take it back, saying, "I must find my favorite card. It's my favorite card, because it never lets me down."

Fan the cards, faces towards you, noting the top and bottom cards. They must be of different suits and values. If they are not, have the cards shuffled again, saying that you want them really well mixed. It is unlikely that you will need them shuffled a third time.

You have noted the top and bottom cards. They will tell you what your favorite card actually is. Suppose that the two cards are the king of clubs and the four of diamonds. Your lucky card will be a combination of these two; it will be either the four of clubs or the king of diamonds. Find one of these and place it face down on the table. "There it is," you say, "my favorite card."

Hold out the deck to the spectator and ask him to cut off a pile. After he does, turn the remaining cards face up in your hand and place your "favorite card" face down on top of the face-up cards. Don't rush it, but do it promptly to keep the spectators from getting a good look at the face-up card. Have the spectator place his pile face up on top of all.

Place the deck face down on the table. Now is the time to give the audience a chance to forget what you just did. Any story will do, but you might want to say something like this: "Why is this particular card my favorite? Years ago I was in a big poker game, and I was way over my head. Only one card would give me the winner—a straight flush. And I got it. Ever since, that has been my favorite card." Pause. "That's a lie. But I need practice with my patter."

Tap the deck for luck. Fan through the face-down cards to your "favorite card." Let us suppose that it is the king of diamonds. Set it and the card on either side of it on the table. Place the rest of the deck aside.

"My favorite card," you say. "And on one side, a card of the same suit. And on the other, a card of the same value." As you say this, turn each of the cards over.

"Now you know the *real* reason it's my favorite card."

Ups and Downs

With this trick, a selected card is found at the precise point a spectator tells the magician to stop dealing.

For years, I tried to work out a good way to do this. There are plenty of ways, but most require advanced sleight of hand and look pretty fishy. One day a few years ago, I stumbled on a very simple method. It is not so simple, however, that it doesn't astonish spectators.

A chosen card must be brought to the top of the deck. A pro would use sleight of hand; we'll try subterfuge.

As I considered various sneaky methods, I recalled a device used in an old trick called *Card from the Pocket*. Combining a variation of this device with my new idea would produce a doubly astonishing trick. A spectator looks at a card at a chosen number down in the deck. The performer causes the card to move from that number to a spot in the deck chosen completely at random by the spectator. Best of all, the working is clean and there is no sleight of hand.

Turn your back and have the spectator shuffle the deck. Say, "I would like you to think of a number from five to twenty. Now count down to that number, taking one card under the other so that you don't reverse their order. Look at the card that lies at that number, show it around, and replace the cards on top."

Turn around and take the deck, saying, "We have a chosen card which lies at a freely selected number down in the deck. Now, quick as a flash, I'm going to move your card to a much more convenient spot."

Place the deck behind your back, move the top card to the bottom, give the ends a noisy riffle, and bring the deck forward. It should take no more than a few seconds.

"All set. But first, let's make sure I *have* moved your card. What number down in the deck was it?"

When he tells you, deal the cards into a pile, one on top of the other, until you get to the chosen number. Deal that card out face up. As you place the dealt pile on top of the deck, say, "Not your card, right?"

Naturally, it is not. Pick up the card and stick it face down into the middle of the deck. The chosen card is now on top.

"I would like you to watch for your card as I deal, but don't say anything if you see it." Deal the cards into a pile. The top card is face down, the second face up, the third face down, the fourth face up, and so on. After you have dealt ten or so, tell the spectator, "Please tell me when to stop."

When he says stop, offer to deal more if he wishes. If he chooses to have you deal more, go ahead. And at the next stop, again offer to deal more. It doesn't matter to you. Just remember to continue the face-down, face-up pattern.

When the spectator stops you, pick up the pile of cards and place them on top of the deck, apparently to straighten up the pile. But by no means comment on this. Fan quickly through the cards to the last face-up card and lift them off (including the last face-up card). Set the rest of the deck down with your left hand. The top card of the deck is, of course, the selected card. As you fan through the cards and lift them off, ask, "Do you see your card among these?" Of course he doesn't.

"Then let's take a look at the face-down ones." Deal the packet into a face-up pile. Face-down cards are turned over and dealt face up; others are simply added to the pile as they are. "Seen your card yet?" He hasn't.

"Are you sure you remember the name of your card?" When he assures you that he does, ask him the name. Nod knowingly and say, "Of course." Tap the top card of the deck and turn it over. "See? I told you I was going to move your card to a much more convenient spot."

Here's a minor point which could make all the difference: When you deal the cards into a face-down, face-up pile, make sure that they overlap enough to conceal that first face-down card, which, of course, is the chosen one.

Spelling _____

Impromptu Speller

With this trick, a card is chosen, shown around, and returned to the deck, which is thoroughly shuffled. Nevertheless, the performer spells out the name of the card (dealing one card from the top for each letter in the spelling), and it appears on the last letter of the spelling.

That's a fairly accurate description of most spelling tricks, including this one. Spelling tricks abound. Most require setups, and many others seem cumbersome. This is one of the best, because it is quick, direct, surprising, and—add to that, easy.

A card is selected by a spectator. You must know the name of this card. I suggest you use the *One-Cut Force* (page 19), or the *Double-Turnover Force* (page 20). Have the spectator show the card around, put it back into the deck, and then shuffle the cards. You also give the cards a good shuffle.

"I know what a suspicious person you are. You know how magical I am, and you think I have sneakily removed your card from the deck. I can assure you that nothing is farther from the truth. Here, I'll show you." Turn the deck face up and begin fanning through the cards, from bottom to top.

"I want you to notice that your card is still here, but don't reveal the card to me by so much as a word or gesture. Just observe that it's still here."

As you fan rapidly through the cards, one by one, watch for the selected card. When you come to it, begin spelling the name of the card to yourself, moving one card (to the right) for each letter in the spelling. Let us say the selected card was the jack of hearts. When you come to it, count it as J, the next card as A, the next C, the next K, until you have spelled J-A-C-K-O-F-H-E-A-R-T-S. Note the very next card. Suppose it is the three of clubs. Spell out that card in the same way. Separate the cards at the point where you complete the spelling. Tap the next card with the cards in your right hand.

"See that card? I can tell you this. That card is *not* your selected card." Cut the deck at the point of the division, bringing the indicated card to the bottom, and turn the deck face down.

"Want to see another trick?" Pause. "Just kidding. No need to get upset. Now I assume you saw your card." The spectator will probably admit it. "Okay. We're going to try to find your card by spelling its name. For example, if your card had been the three of clubs (name the second card you mentally spelled out), we would spell it like this."

Spell out the name of the card, dealing out one card from the top for each letter in the spelling. On the last card of the spelling, turn the card over. It is the card you spelled—in our example, the three of clubs.

"There you are—the three of clubs. We will try to find your card the same way. What was the name of your card?"

He names it, and you spell it out, revealing his chosen card on the last letter of the spelling.

Note: When you are going through the deck, showing the spectator that his card is still there, you will sometimes find that his card is near the top. Just continue the count from the bottom, saying, "Funny, I haven't seen your card yet," or something equally inane.

Quick Speller

Ready for a paradox? In performance, this is one of the shortest tricks in the book. Naturally, it has the longest description. Stick with me on this one. The trick will seem a little complicated at first—actually it is not. You may find that this will be one of your favorites.

The trick is old but still good. Unfortunately, some versions are complicated and unnatural. All versions seem to require considerable memorization. My variation is simple and natural, and you need to remember only a few things.

First, the simple explanation. Every card in the deck can be spelled out, one way or another, in twelve cards, either by turning over the last card of the spelling or by turning over the next card. So the performer simply arranges for the chosen card to be twelfth from the top.

Here's an easy way to get it twelfth down. Have the deck shuffled. Take it back and give four cards to each of three spectators. Have each one remove a card from his group of four. A fourth spectator takes one of these three cards, shows it to everyone but you, and places it on top of the deck.

"Thus," you say, as you gather up the eleven outstanding cards, "we guarantee a card chosen completely at random." Place the eleven cards on top and proceed with a false cut (*The One-Finger Cut*, on page 21).

You ask the spectator to name his card. He does. You spell it out, dealing off one card for each letter—and there's his card. It's not quite that simple, of course, but not as difficult as some card writers have tried to make out. I will tell you exactly how I taught myself to spell out all the cards.

The most important thing to remember is that the card is twelfth from the top. This means that if the selected card spells out in twelve letters, you turn over the last card of the spelling. If it spells out in eleven letters, you spell out the card and turn over the *next* card. Exactly twenty-seven cards spell out in eleven or twelve letters. Not bad—but others you have to work at a little.

How about cards that spell out in ten letters? There are only four, and they are all clubs. Obviously, when you finish spelling out the card's name, the chosen card will still be two down in the deck. No problem. Before you start spelling, you will lose a card from the top—it's easy, as I will explain later—and turn over the next card after completing the spelling.

Seventeen cards are spelled with thirteen or fourteen letters. We eliminate the two letters in "of" by spelling out the suit and then the value. Now they can be handled exactly the same as cards that spell out with eleven or twelve letters. With twelve letters (originally fourteen), you turn over the last card of the spelling; with eleven (originally thirteen), you turn over the next card.

Only four cards, all diamonds, spell out in fifteen letters. These require special handling, as I will explain later.

Does it sound too complicated? Actually, you need remember very little of the above. The spectator names his card, and you have it twelfth from the top. Somehow you must get to that twelfth card. This requires a quick computation. While figuring out how I'm going to spell out the card, I usually make small talk, saying things like, "Oh, the king of spades. That's one of my favorite cards. I see no reason this shouldn't work out perfectly."

How do I compute? The easiest way, I have discovered, is to first figure the suit and then the value. Clubs count five, spades and hearts six, and diamonds eight. *That* you should remember. Values count three, four or five. That you *don't* have to remember.

Let's take a few examples. The spectator names the seven of hearts. Hearts is six, seven is five. That's eleven. Add two more for "of." That's thirteen. No good. We'll have to spell out H-E-A-R-T-S and then S-E-V-E-N, and turn up the *next* card.

The spectator names the jack of spades. Spades is six; jack is four. Add two more for the "of." That's twelve. Spell out J-A-C-K-O-F-S-P-A-D-E-S, and turn over the last card of the spelling.

I will make a suggestion soon that will make all of this second nature to you. First, let's go over how you handle the spellings. As I mentioned, with cards that spell out in eleven or twelve letters, you simply spell out the card. With a card that spells in eleven letters, you spell out the card and turn over the next card. With a card that spells out in twelve letters, you turn over the last card of the spelling.

With cards that spell out to thirteen or fourteen letters, eliminate the "of." Then treat them exactly like cards that spell out in eleven or twelve letters.

Let's try thirteen. The spectator says the queen of hearts is his card. You see that hearts is six and queen is five. Add two more for "of." You have thirteen. Drop the "of" and you have eleven letters. Although you have already been told the name of the card, you now say to the spectator, "Let's see— what's the suit?" He will say, "Hearts." You spell it out.

"And what's the value?" you ask. He says, "Queen." So you spell it out *and turn over the next card.*

Suppose the number is fourteen. Diamonds is the only suit in which cards are spelled out in fourteen or fifteen letters. For fourteen letters, you follow the same procedure as with thirteen, only you turn over the *last card of the spelling.*

Only four cards are spelled out with fifteen letters. You follow a procedure similar to that used for thirteen- and fourteen-letter cards. Drop the word "of," spelling out the suit and then the value. But that means you will have dealt one beyond the card when you spell it out.

So you must get rid of one letter in the spelling. You do that by getting rid of the "s" at the end of "diamonds" with a little verbal trick. It will seem perfectly natural if you follow the precise wording. Suppose that the spectator says his card is the seven of diamonds. You note diamonds is eight, and seven is five. That's thirteen—already too high. You say, "Let's see. Your card is a diamond." Spell out diamond. "And the value is what?"

He says, "Seven." Spell out seven, turning over the last card of the spelling.

Just keep remembering the card is twelfth down; the rest is easy.

But how about the cards that spell out in ten letters? As I mentioned, there are only four, all clubs. You must lose a card from the top, bringing the chosen card eleventh from the top. Now you can spell it out and turn over the next card.

How do you lose a card from the top? I do it the easy way. After the spectator names his card, and I note that it spells out in ten, I show the top card, saying, "Your card is not on top," and I bury it in the middle. Immediately, as a smoke screen, I add, "And your card is not on the bottom," and I show it and bury it in the middle. Then I proceed with the spelling.

Now for the suggestion that will make all this second nature to you. Go through the entire deck, figuring out the spelling of each card. Here's the way I do it. I count off eleven cards, look at the bottom card of the deck and place it below the eleven cards, which I return to the top. The card is now twelfth down.

I proceed exactly as though a spectator were there. I make small talk while I compute the spelling of the card, *and then I spell it out.* I discard that one. Eleven cards are already counted off, so I look at the bottom card of the deck, place it below the eleven cards, place all on top, and proceed as before.

When I finish the deck, there are still eleven cards not spelled out. I set these aside, and then take the rest of the deck, count off eleven, take a look at one of the eleven I used in the preceding spellings, place it below the new pile of eleven, and place all on top of the deck. Then I spell the card out, as before. I do the same with the remaining ten.

Incidentally, the spelling of some cards differently is *not* a drawback. Since the spectator doesn't know what to expect, and since you perform the trick only once, the effect is perfect.

Review of the actual spelling: The spectator's card is twelfth from the top. The card's name can be made up of ten, eleven, twelve, thirteen, fourteen, or fifteen letters.

Ten letters. Only four cards, all clubs, spell out in ten letters. Before spelling, you must lose a card from the top. You do this by showing that the top and bottom cards are not the chosen ones and then burying them in the middle. Now you spell out the card and turn over the *next* card.

Eleven letters. Spell the card out and turn over the *next* card.

Twelve letters. Spell the card out and turn over the *last* card.

Thirteen letters. Spell out the suit (including the "s" at the end) and then the value. Drop the word "of." Turn over the *next* card.

Fourteen letters. Only five cards, all diamonds, are spelled out in fourteen letters. Spell out the suit (including the "s" at the end) and then the value. Turn over the *last* card.

Fifteen letters. Only four cards, all diamonds, are spelled out in fifteen letters. You say, "Your card is a diamond." Spell out "diamond" without the "s" at the end. Then spell out the value. Turn over the last card of the spelling.

Why have I gone into such detail with this particular trick when others seem easier? Because it is the best, the fastest, and the most direct of all spelling tricks.

A Hot Spell

An old principle is used in this trick. In fact, I use a variation of this principle in *Tick Tock Trick*; but I felt there had to be at least one more good effect using the same principle—all it would take was camouflage. I came up with this spelling trick, which gets excellent audience response.

Have a volunteer shuffle the deck as you explain, "I am going to attempt a feat of mentalism. Would you please think of a number from one to ten. Do you have one? All right. Now change your mind. This is not psychological; we must be sure you have complete freedom of choice.

"In a moment I'll turn my back, and I would like you to count two piles of cards, both containing the same number of cards as the number you thought of. For example, if you thought of four, deal two piles of cards with four cards in each pile. Do this quietly so I won't be able to hear you." Turn away while the spectator follows your instructions.

"Now lift up either of the two piles, look at the bottom card, and show it around. Please remember that card. And now place that pile on top of the deck." After your assistant is done, continue, "Please place the deck in my hand and hide the other pile you dealt."

Turn around and face the spectators with the pack behind your back and say, "I am going to find your card *behind my back*, using nothing more than mental vibrations to guide me. What's your card?"

When the spectator names his card, spell it, removing one card from the top for each letter, like this: Suppose the spectator says his card was the nine of clubs. You mentally say "N" and take the top card in your right hand. For the letter "I", you take the next card on top of the first. The card for "N" goes on top of the first two. The card for "E" goes on top of the first three. Continue on, adding one card on top of those in the right hand for each letter remaining in the spelling: O-F-C-L-U-B-S.

Naturally, you do not want the spectators to *hear* you doing this, and you do not want to give away the fact that you are doing anything tricky with the deck. The counting of one card on top of the other must be done fairly slowly; otherwise, noise will give it away. So take your time. You can do what I do: Babble while spelling out the card.

I spell the card out in three chunks. With our example, I would spell the nine of clubs like this: While spelling N-I-N-E, taking one card in my right hand for each letter, I would say something like "Nine . . . nine . . . very difficult. Really think of the value nine, so that I can feel that card vibrating." By this time, I have four cards in my right hand. I add two more for O-F, while saying something like "I'm not sure. I may have it." Then, while spelling C-L-U-B-S, I might say, "Nine of clubs is very tough. Clubs, clubs, clubs. Particularly confusing." Notice that this sort of jabbering helps you keep track of what you are doing behind your back, while creating the illusion that you are either a mentalist or a lunatic.

Bring the deck forward and say, "Presto! Here is your card, right on top." Turn over the top card. It is wrong, of course. You place the card in the middle of the deck, declaring, "Of course that isn't your card. I know what's wrong. It's what people always say about me: 'He's not playing with a full deck.' Would you please put the rest of the cards on top. I won't look."

Avert your head while your assistant puts on top of the deck the pile of cards he had hidden. Take the deck and hold it to your forehead, saying, "Concentrate on your card, please." After a moment of intense thinking, say, "I know exactly how to find your card. We'll spell it out. What is your card, please?" Yes, he has told you the name already, but there is no need to stress that.

When he names his card, spell it out, dealing one card from the top for each letter in the spelling. Turn the last card of the spelling face up; it is the spectator's card.

Gambling

Two-Handed Poker

After doing a number of card tricks, you will frequently hear, "I'd sure hate to play poker with you," or, "Could you cheat at poker?" It's not a bad idea, then, to have a poker trick in your arsenal. This one is very easy and very clever.

You offer to demonstrate crooked poker dealing. But to make things easier, you will use only ten cards. Remove from the deck three aces, three kings, three tens, and a nine. Don't show them. Have the nine on top.

With an overhand shuffle, draw off the nine and shuffle the rest of the cards on top of it. Shuffle again, drawing off the last few cards singly so that the nine ends on top. If you cannot do the overhand shuffle, simply mess the cards around on the table and then gather them up, making sure that the nine ends on top. You may follow this procedure for all succeeding deals.

Deal the cards alternately to the spectator and yourself. Naturally, when the hands are turned over, you win.

This is one of the most ingenious poker effects ever devised. The fact is, the hand with the nine can never win. Is that cute, or what? Take the nine and try getting a winning hand with any four other cards of the nine cards remaining. If you take two pairs, the other hand will have three of a kind. If you take three of a kind, the other hand will be a full house. If you take a pair, the other hand will have two pairs.

Repeat the trick a few times. Then, with a shuffle, leave the nine on the bottom and let the spectator deal. He loses, of course.

Next, shuffle the nine to the top. Hand the deck to the spectator and tell him that you will try something different. "You may deal the cards one at a time to either hand in any order you wish—just so we both end up with five." If the spectator deals the first card to himself, he loses, so try the stunt again. Say, "Deal them in any order you wish."

If the first card goes to you, say, "Now *this* time, no matter what you do, *I* am going to lose."

If the spectator insists on dealing the first card to himself two or three times, you'd better hang up. You are simply destined to win. Gather up the cards, toss them on the deck, and shuffle. After all, we mustn't call attention to that nine. Don't be afraid to repeat this trick. Over the years, I've never had anyone catch on.

Gambler's Bonus

Here is a routine of four gambling tricks, guaranteed to convince onlookers that you are one skilled prestidigitator. No sleight is ever involved.

When you do a gambling demonstration, you are in a paradoxical position. During most of your tricks, you are trying to convince spectators that it is all magic, that you use no sleight of hand. With a gambling demonstration, however, you attempt to show how skilfully you manipulate the cards. In the first instance, you may be using plenty of sleights; in the second, you will be using none.

When you do your tricks, what are the spectators to believe? At one level, they *know* that you are using all sorts of skullduggery, probably including sleights. But if they are to enjoy your performance, they must suspend their disbelief. In a sense, they *want* to believe in magic; often, the more skeptical a spectator seems, the more he wants to believe. To most spectators, you are Mr. or Ms. Magic; the fact that you have displayed apparent manipulative ability with the cards in a gambling routine will add to this illusion.

These tricks are arranged to facilitate going from one to the next; I recommend that you try the whole routine a few times before selecting a favorite or two.

Mind Control Poker

Ask for the help of an assistant. Tell the volunteer, "I am going to set up some cards and then attempt to control your mind in a little poker demonstration."

The setup takes very little time. Hold the card faces towards you and thumb through them, finding the appropriate cards. First, find a king; separate the cards at that point so that the king is the rearmost card of those in your right hand. Take the king behind the cards in the left hand, using the left fingers to grasp it. Thus, the king becomes the top card of the deck. Find an ace and place it on top of the king. Continue by placing on top two nines, two queens, two jacks, two tens, and a king.

From the bottom up, the eleven cards are K-A-9-9-Q-Q-J-J-10-10-K. The last king is the top card. Here is an easy way to remember this stack. I remember KANN, as in "I think I KANN." This gives me the first four cards I must put on top: K (king), A (ace), N (nine), N (nine). I have no trouble remembering the next three pairs—queens, jacks, tens—because they are in descending order. Last, a king goes on top.

Turn the deck face down and say that you're all set. "Obviously, we'll need some cards." Count off eleven cards from the top of the deck, taking them one under the other so that they retain the same order. Make no mention of the number. A good way to count them off is to take three groups of three and one group of two into the right hand. Set the rest of the deck down.

"Now you're going to choose from five sets of two cards," you say. Take the top two cards of your packet (a king and a ten) and spread them, showing them to the spectator. Make no comment about the values of the cards. Place these two cards together on the bottom of the packet, keeping them in their original order. Show the next pair in the same way. Continue on until you have shown the spectator five pairs of cards, each time placing the pair on the bottom.

"Now I am going to offer you a choice. But there really is no choice at all. I am going to control your mind so that you will end up with a *king high straight*. No doubt of it; you will choose a king high straight."

Take the top two cards and spread them slightly, face down, offering the spectator his choice of the two. "Take either one," you say, "and place it face down in front of you." After he chooses one, place the other card on the bottom.

If you have been following this with cards in your hand, take a look at your packet. You will notice that in each instance you are offering him the choice of a pair. His first choice, for instance, is from a pair of kings. Obviously, this is because you actually started with eleven cards, not ten. For whatever reason, spectators never suspect.

Again you take two cards from the top of the packet and offer the spectator his choice. Place the rejected card on the bottom. Continue on until the spectator has chosen five cards. Each time you have placed the remaining card on the bottom. This includes the last choice. Place your packet of six cards on top of the deck.

"Five different times you had complete freedom of choice," you explain, "but I still controlled your mind. Take a look at what you have."

When the spectator shows his cards, he reveals a king high straight, just as you had predicted. Give everyone a chance to verify this and then say, "That wouldn't do you much good, though. Look what you left me."

Take five cards from the top of the deck and show that you have an *ace high straight*. Before I display them, I generally adjust the cards so that they read in A-K-Q-J-10 order.

Flush of Success

You explain that you are going to demonstrate how easy it is to get a good hand when you have all the best cards to choose from. As you chat on, remove all the high cards from the deck: aces, kings, queens, jacks, and tens. You may fan through the cards and toss them out face up as you come to them. You may try this method, which is faster: Fan through the cards and when you come to one of the high cards, push it upwards about an inch so that it sticks out of the top of the deck. Do the same with all the other high cards. When done, turn the deck face down, grasp all the protruding cards at the side, and pull them from the deck.

Spread all the high cards out face up on the table. What you are about to do is lay out four hands, arranging it so that you will get a *royal flush in hearts* when the cards are gathered together and dealt.

As I will explain, you improvise with the spectators as you lay out the four hands face up. In the first hand, the second card must be a heart. Since the hands are laid out face up, we are talking about the fourth card down as the cards lie face up, or the *second card* if the hand were turned face down and dealt.

In the second hand, a heart must be placed third. In the next hand, a heart must be placed fourth. And in the last hand, a heart must be placed first and fifth.

In the first hand, a heart is second; in the second hand, a heart is third; in the third hand, a heart is fourth; and in the fourth hand, a heart is at both top and bottom.

Pick up the hands face up in this order: The fourth hand goes on the first hand; this pile goes on the second hand; that pile goes on the third hand. Turn the packet face down and give the cards a complete cut.

Spectators tend to believe that a complete cut disarranges the cards. Actually, the cards are in a never ending sequence, and a cut retains their order. If you were to cut the original top card back to the top, the packet would be in precisely the same order as before the cutting started.

Have various spectators give the cards a complete cut. For the trick to work, you must have a heart on the bottom. So after each cut is completed, grasp the deck edgeways, tilt it up so that you can see the face of the bottom card, and tap the cards on the table as though straightening them out. If the bottom card is other than a heart, have the cards cut again. Repeat this until you get a heart on the bottom.

Then deal four face-down poker hands, including one to yourself. Show the first hand, commenting on its value. Show the second and third hands the same way. Say, "It really doesn't matter. It's pretty hard to beat a royal flush." Turn your hand over and show it. Again, I like to arrange the cards from ace to ten before showing the hand.

How do you improvise with the spectators as you make up the hands? You might say something like, "Look at all these great cards. What would be a pretty good hand?"

If a spectator calls for a flush or a straight flush, you cannot oblige, for the first hand must have precisely one heart. So you might say, "Not *that* good!"

Chances are you'll be asked for two pairs, three of a kind, or a straight. Make up the hand from the spread-out cards, making sure that the second card is a heart, and that no other is. Put together the next two hands the same way. Spectators will probably want one of them to be a full house. If they again ask for a flush, say, "Sure, just watch my face if this doesn't work."

Take up the last five cards on the table; quite often they will make up a pretty good hand. Make sure you have a heart on top and a heart on bottom.

You'll have little trouble providing the hands called for; after all, the spectators must choose from the cards on the table. You can have a lot of fun improvising with the spectators.

You can also get some entertainment from the repeated cuts as you keep looking for a heart at the bottom of the stack before you deal. Sometimes the number of cuts can go to double figures before a heart finally shows up at the bottom. This can be turned to your advantage, as you say things like, "Let's try one more cut, just to make sure they're mixed." Or, "Let's try one with the left hand." You can ad-lib other equally inane reasons. When you finally get a heart on the bottom, you can say, "I don't know about you, but I'm getting sick of this." Take the cards and deal the hands.

Gambling Aces

A simple stack is required for the next trick. You can cleverly cover this up by saying, "I have to stack these cards . . . hope you don't mind." Thumb through the cards and, following the procedure described in *Mind Control Poker* (page 75), place three nines on top. Place five spot cards on top of them. Now from the top down, you have five spot cards followed by three nines.

Mutter something like, "Now where the heck are those aces?" Find the aces and place them on top one by one in the manner described. "All set." From the top down you have four aces, five spot cards, three nines.

Commence your patter: "A cardsharp was attending a quiet party when he decided to liven things up a bit. He slapped a deck of cards down on a table . . ." Slap the deck down on the table. ". . . and said, 'Who wants to play three-handed poker?'"

"Naturally, everyone gathered around. A wise guy asked, 'Why three-handed poker?' The cardsharp told him, 'To make it easier.' The wise guy said, 'I've seen this before. Where are the four aces?' The cardsharp said, 'Right here on top—just in case I need them.'" Deal out the four aces face up.

"The cardsharp said, 'Now I'll deal a few sample hands before we start the betting.'" Put the aces back on top. Deal four hands of three cards each, including one hand to yourself.

"The wise guy said, 'You just stacked the cards so you'd get three aces.' The cardsharp said, 'Not at all. Look—one ace in each hand.'"

Pick up your hand and turn it over, showing that there is only one ace. Place the hand on top. Do the same with the third hand, the second hand, and the first hand, in that order—each time placing the hand on top.

"The cardsharp said, 'Let's try another deal.' " Again deal four hands of three cards each.

"The wise guy said, 'I've seen this. For sure, you've stacked them this time.' The cardsharp said, 'No way. Look—one ace in each hand.' " Show the hands in precisely the same way as you did the first time.

"The cardsharp said, 'Now let's get down to business. One more deal.' " Deal four hands of three cards each.

"The cardsharp asked, 'Now who wants to make a bet?' The wise guy said, *"I'll* make a bet. You stacked the cards. I'll bet you twenty bucks you hold three aces.' The cardsharp said, 'You're on, buddy. And you're dead wrong.' "

Move your three-card hand to one side. *Now this is important*: Place the third hand on top of the deck, followed by the second hand and the first hand.

"The cardsharp said, 'You're right about one thing—I did stack the cards.' " Turn over your hand, showing the three nines.

"The wise guy forked over the twenty and said, 'What about the aces?' The cardsharp smiled and said, 'I told you. Right here on top—just in case I need them.' " As you say this, deal the aces face up one by one. Just follow the directions; the trick works itself.

At the conclusion of the trick, replace the aces on top and give the cards a casual overhand shuffle, bringing them to the middle. You'll need them for the next trick.

Ace Surprise

You will need the four aces on top. At the end of *Gambling Aces* (page 81), you shuffled them to the middle. As you commence your patter, begin fanning through the cards, faces towards you. You will be looking for the four kings, but in your first move, simply cut the aces to the top and continue fanning through the cards.

"I'll need the four kings for this," you say as you begin going through the deck. "This is my last gambling demonstration and you may be able to catch me if you watch very carefully." Toss out the kings face up as you come to them. "Some gamblers can deal seconds, some can deal thirds, some can deal bottoms, and some can deal cards from the middle. And a good cheater makes it look as though they are all coming from the top."

You should have the kings face up on the table now. "I'm not going to tell you exactly what trickery I'm up to, but I urge you to watch closely."

Gather up the kings and place them on top. Even up the cards carefully and deal them out face down next to one another. "Are these the four kings?" Pause. "Of course they are."

As you show each one, place it back on top. Then deal the kings out again face down. "Four kings. Now watch."

From here on, do *not* describe what you are doing. Fan out four cards from the top of the deck, taking them in the right hand. Tilt the deck down slightly with the left hand and square up the cards against the base of the left thumb. Drop these four on top of the first king you dealt out, the one to your left. Even up this pile meticulously and place it on top of the deck. Even up the deck. Carefully deal the top card face down, well off to your left.

Again fan out the four top cards, taking them in your right hand and squaring them against the base of your left thumb. Drop these four on top of the second king you dealt. Even up the pile and place it on top. Square up the deck. Deliberately deal the top card face down on the one you already dealt to your far left. Follow the same procedure with the two remaining kings. Then set the deck down to your right.

"Were you watching carefully? I hope so. The question is, 'Where are the kings?'" Chances are that the spectators will say that the kings are on the pile you dealt to your left. If they do, say, "Oh, no. The kings are right here." Deal them face up one at a time off the top of the deck. "There's a much better hand over here." Deal the four-card pile face up one at a time, revealing the four aces.

If the spectators should indicate that the four kings are on top of the deck, show them that this is so by dealing them out face up. "You're right. These are the kings. But what good are kings . . ." Deal the four-card pile face up. ". . . against four aces?"

Grab Bag

Countdown

The principle used in this trick is old, deceptive, and applicable to any number of tricks. A card is selected and returned to the deck. The spectator locates his own card by counting off a freely selected number of cards. This is the general effect.

Actually, a card is forced on a spectator. See *One-Cut Force* (page 19), *Double-Turnover Force* (page 20), or *Face-Up Force* (page 19). After the spectator shows the card around, he returns it to the deck and shuffles the cards.

Taking the deck back, you say, "Now watch how I do this." Fan through the cards, faces towards you. When you come to the selected card, count off nine cards beyond and cut the deck at that point. The selected card is now ten down from the top.

Show the spectators the bottom card, declaring triumphantly, *"This* is not your card." After the excitement dies down, add, "I could do that trick forever. But let's see how you can do."

Give him the deck and tell him to deal into a pile any number of cards from ten to twenty. Tell him to add the digits of his selected number and to deal that number back on top of the deck. For instance, if he dealt off thirteen cards, he adds one and three, and deals four cards back onto the deck.

"What is the name of your card?" you ask.

When he names it, you turn over the last card dealt back on the deck. Sure enough.

Clearly, it doesn't matter what number from ten to twenty is chosen. When the digits are totalled and the sum counted back onto the deck, the original tenth card down will be the last card dealt.

The Four Aces Again

This trick is based on the same principle as *Count-down*. The effect is so astonishing that I suspend my prejudice against setups. Besides, the setup can be done with the spectators watching.

The setup is this: You need the four aces to be tenth, eleventh, twelfth, and thirteenth from the top of the deck. If you're using your own deck, you can set up the cards in advance and make this your first trick. After I explain how the trick works, I will give you two impromptu methods of setting up the cards.

The strong point to this trick is that the spectator does it all. Tell him to think of any number from ten to twenty and to deal that number of cards into a pile. Then he is to add the digits in the number and deal that many cards back onto the deck. When he is done, take the cards remaining in his dealt hand and set them aside.

"Now I would like you to deal the remaining cards one at a time into four neat piles, just as though you were dealing hands."

The first four cards he deals are, of course, the aces; they will be at the bottom of the four piles. After he has dealt twenty or so cards, tell him, "You may deal as many more as you want and stop whenever you wish." When he stops, take the remaining cards from him and add them to the others you originally set aside.

At this point, a little review should add to the mystification. "You freely selected the original number you dealt off. And when you dealt the cards, you stopped wherever you wished. Right?"

Don't wait for an answer. Simply turn over all four piles, displaying an ace at the face of each.

As promised, here's a way to set up the cards while the spectators watch. Suppose you have just performed a four-aces trick, like *Easy Aces* (page 40). When you are finished, make sure the aces are together in the deck. Do a few more tricks, preferably ones which do not call for shuffling. Fan through the cards, faces towards you. When you come to the four aces, count nine cards beyond. Part the deck at this point and cut them. This brings the aces to the desired position from the top. Show the bottom card, saying, "This is *your* good-luck card. Let's see if it works."

Apparently, you have simply looked through the deck and found his good-luck card and cut it to the bottom. Take off the good-luck card and set it to one side. Before the climax, you can wave the card over the four piles to help bring about the magical result.

Suppose the aces are scattered through the deck. Again run through the cards, faces towards you. Tell the spectators that you must find *precisely* the right card for the experiment to work.

As you come to each ace, separate the cards and thumb each ace to the bottom. "No, no," you mumble, as you keep adding aces to the bottom. When all four are on the bottom, go back to fan through again. As before, count nine cards beyond the aces and cut the cards at that point.

Show the bottom card. "Here it is!" you declare, setting the card aside. "Without this bad-luck card, the experiment is bound to work."

Get Out of This World

When I was young (back in the olden days), this trick was called *Out of This World*. Many feel it is the best card trick ever invented.

With the deck face down, the spectator attempts to separate the red and black cards. To his amazement, he succeeds. The problem is that the trick requires a completely set-up deck. Lots of us worked out ways to set up the deck in the course of doing other tricks, but at best they were clumsy, and they were always a pain in the neck to the performer.

Here is an impromptu method that many lay claim to. All I have added are a few tips. The virtues to this method are:

1. There are no sleights whatsoever.

2. There is no prearrangement of the cards.

3. It is *snappy*. Furthermore, the effect is astonishing.

"For this experiment," you tell the spectators, "I need an assistant, preferably one with ESP or psychic powers. If we can't manage that, I'll settle for someone who's heard of ESP or psychic powers. Or I'll take someone who can *spell* ESP."

When you get your volunteer, have him shuffle the deck and hand it back to you. Fan the cards in your left hand, faces towards you, making sure that the spectators do not see the faces. Now you are going to eliminate all of one color from the top three-fifths or so of the deck. You will do this by taking them out one by one, as I will explain in a moment. This will leave you with a top section of approximately fifteen to twenty cards of the opposite color.

Look over the top section and see which color dominates. You must eliminate the opposite color. For example, if there are more reds than blacks in the top portion of the deck, you will want to take out all of the blacks and leave the reds. Let's assume that this is the case: You want to get rid of the blacks. Take a black card from the top portion and place it face up on the table. Next to it place a face-up red card that you get from the bottom portion of the deck.

"These are the markers," you explain. "If you think a card is red, we'll place it on the red marker. If you think it is black, we'll place it on the black

Illus. 10. This is the spectator's view of the two overlapping columns, with the two markers, one red, one black.

marker. This way we'll discover whether you have any extrasensory perception."

Pick out a black card from the top portion of the fanned cards. Holding it face down, ask the spectator, "Do you think this one is red or black?" When he answers, place it face down on the appropriate marker. Continue in the same way, eliminating black cards from the top section of the deck.

Place the cards on the table in an overlapping column going away from you. From the spectator's view, the cards will look like Illus. 10.

Pretend to study the cards as you pick one out for the spectator's decision. Playact. You are pleased with some of his choices; you frown slightly at others. Tell your assistant, "You're doing quite well for an amateur."

As an added fillip, you can do this: When the spectator calls black, smile, and show him the card before you place it on the black pile. Compliment him. Do this once only, of course.

When you have fifteen or more cards of the opposite color in the top portion of the deck (in our example, red), stop the deal. "I think your psychic vibrations are fading from boredom; we must try something a little different."

Hand the spectator the bottom portion of the remaining deck and keep the top portion (the cards of one color) for yourself. Tell him to shuffle his pile. While he does so, shuffle your pile.

Exchange piles with the spectator. Shuffle your pile and tell him to shuffle his. Since his are all of the same color, the shuffle will obviously not affect the outcome.

Take a red card from your pile and place it face up on the black pile. Take a black card from your pile and place it face up on the red pile. Set aside your pile without comment.

"From now on, black cards go here . . ." Indicate the new black marker. ". . . and red cards go here." Indicate the new red marker. "Now I'd just as soon you do your own dealing. I'm exhausted. Just go through one card at a time, dealing face down, and follow your instincts."

You may try another bit of byplay if you wish. When the spectator has dealt about half of the cards, stop him, saying, "Oh-oh!" Take the last dealt card from the black pile. It is, of course, a red card. Show the card and place it face down on the red pile, saying, "I wish you'd be a little more careful." The cards should be lined up as in Illus. 11.

When the spectator finishes, one column of cards is perfect: The black cards are under the black marker, and the red cards are under the red. The other pile, however, has black cards under the red marker, and red cards under the black. In the original version, a sleight was recommended to enable the performer to show the second pile to be perfect. No sleight is necessary. The method of showing the piles given here is totally deceptive and has the added advantage of not appearing suspicious.

When the spectator finishes dealing, go to the "good" pile. Separate the reds from the blacks by leaving an inch or two at the middle marker. Remove the two markers and casually toss them aside, face down. Turn over the color group closest to the spectators, spreading the cards sideways to show they are all the same color. Then turn over the group nearest you and spread the cards sideways (nearer to you than your first spread), showing that they, too, are all of the same color (Illus. 12).

Illus. 11.   The cards should be lined up as shown above. Two new markers have been dealt.

Handle the other pile just as casually. Close it and pick it up. Turn it over so that the cards are face up and the two markers are face down. Casually discard the marker that was on top, putting it with the other two markers you have discarded. Fan the cards down to the next marker, showing them to be the same color. Remove this group, still fanned out, and place it next to the pile on the table closest to the spectators. The two groups nearest the spectators are of opposite colors (Illus. 13).

Illus. 12.   Turn over the group nearest you and spread the cards sideways (nearer to you than your first spread). Show that this group, too, is all of the same color.

Illus. 13.   The two groups nearest the spectators are of opposite colors.

Discard the fourth marker, placing it with the other three markers. Fan the remaining cards, showing that they are the same color. Place this group, still spread out, next to the group nearest you. Everything is perfect. Reds are next to blacks, just as (presumably) they were dealt.

Pick up the markers, casually add them to the discarded pile. Give the pile a little shuffle; then congratulate the spectator on his extraordinary powers as you gather up the rest of the cards.

Go over this one several times before you try it out. You will be pleased with the reaction to "the world's greatest card trick."

The Process of Elimination

Ordinarily, I dislike tricks with a lot of dealing. But done snappily, this one has a tremendous effect.

You say, "I want you to observe how rapidly I deal these cards. It's well known that I'm among the top five percent of rapid card dealers. Which is a real money-making skill. Big call for that."

Rapidly deal six piles of five cards each, thirty cards in all. Have a spectator choose two cards from the remaining deck. Set the rest of the deck aside. Take the two cards and show them to everyone, naming them and making sure to repeat their names at least twice, so that everyone will remember them.

Give the two cards back to the spectator. Tell him, "Please place one of your two chosen cards on top of one of the six piles." After he has done so, say, "Now place the other selected card on top of one of the other piles."

Take note of which two packets have the chosen cards on top. Place two other piles on top of each one. You now have two piles, sixteen cards in each one. In each pile, a chosen card is sixth from the bottom. Place either pile on top of the other.

Next, you will rapidly deal the cards alternately into two piles. Both chosen cards will be in the first pile you deal to. You will eliminate the other pile, as I will explain later.

You will repeat this procedure three times, leaving you with one pile containing two cards. They are, of course, the chosen ones.

Before we go into the elimination process, let us consider the dealing of the cards into two piles. It is not particularly deceptive if you *always* keep the pile on your left. Therefore, I recommend that on the first deal, you start with a card to your left, then one to the right, and so on. The next deal, place the first card to your *right*, the next to the left, and so on. On the third deal, start on your left; on the fourth, start on your right.

Clearly, the entire effect depends upon how you eliminate the piles. You ostensibly offer freedom of choice, while actually keeping the pile you want. Here is what I recommend.

After the first deal, tell the spectator, "Please pick up a pile." If he picks up the pile containing the two chosen cards, take the pile from him and, after brushing the other packet aside, deal the "chosen" pile into two new piles. If he picks up the other pile, take the one he leaves and rapidly deal that one into two piles. When you are done, casually take the pile from him and toss it aside.

After the second deal, tell the spectator, "Please hand me a pile." If he hands you the pile containing the chosen cards, brush the other packet aside, and deal the selected pile into two new piles. If he hands you the other pile, set it aside, pick up the pile with the selected cards, and deal it into two packets.

When you have finished the third deal, ask the spectator, "Which pile?" If he indicates the one containing the chosen cards, push the other packet aside, and deal the chosen pile into two new piles. If he chooses the other one, set it aside, pick up the pile with the selected cards, and deal it into two piles.

On the last deal, you have two packets containing two cards each. Tell the spectator to place a hand on each pile. Then direct him to lift up one hand. If he lifts the hand covering the chosen cards, take that pile and show the cards. If he lifts the other hand, take the pile he uncovers and set it aside. Then show the two selected cards.

The dealing and choosing actually take very little time. And the denouement is quite effective. But for the trick to work, I highly recommend that you follow my instructions for pile selection *precisely*, and please use the exact wording.

First: "Please pick up a pile."
Second: "Please hand me a pile."
Third: "Which pile?"
On the fourth selection, the wording is not critical. Simply tell him to place a hand on each pile.

I remember the order of selection for the first three picks with the words "pick, hand, which." Generally, I can remember the method of doing the last selection.

The Double-Match Trick

This one has to do with matches only in the sense of two things resembling each other. I wish I knew who invented this trick so that I could offer him my heartiest congratulations. It has everything: directness, cleverness, undetectability, and an astonishing climax. What's more, it's easy to execute. And since the spectator does all the work, he is completely mystified. I'm sure this trick will become one of your favorites.

Like most tricks, this one is enhanced by a little romance. "For this experiment," you say, "I need a kindred spirit, someone whose spiritual vibrations will correspond to mine." If no one volunteers, say, "I'll settle for someone who knows one card from the other."

Have your volunteer shuffle the deck. Take it back and fan the cards so that only you can see the faces. "Now I'm going to select two cards, and it's important that I concentrate." As you give the cards a casual fanning, indicating the importance of concentrating, note the top card. Find the card that matches it in color and value, and toss it out face up.

For instance, if the top card is the six of clubs, find the six of spades and toss it out.

Now note the bottom card, find the card that matches it in color and value, and toss that one out face up. Have this one a little closer to you, so you'll remember to use it first.

"I would like you to look at these two cards and try to get a clear impression of them in your mind."

Hand the volunteer the deck and tell him to deal the cards into a face-down pile. After he has dealt a dozen or so cards, tell him to stop whenever he wishes. When he stops dealing, place the *second* card you took from the deck (the one matching the bottom card) face up on top of the pile he dealt from. Tell him to put the rest of the deck on top. You can also point to the second card you took and have the spectator place it face up on top of his dealt cards. This keeps the entire trick in his hands.

The position now is that in the lower portion of the deck your face-up card is face-to-face with its matching card. The bottom card of the deck matches the card on the table.

Again have the spectator deal cards from the top into a face-down pile. When he has dealt a dozen or so, tell him to stop when he wants to. Obviously, he must not deal so many that he gets to the face-up card. If he seems intent on dealing forever, simply take the cards from him and hand them to someone else to complete the deal.

When the spectator stops dealing, place the other face-up card on top of the pile he dealt, or have the spectator do so. The spectator places the rest of the deck on top.

"Now let's see if we are really *simpatico*." Take the deck and very deliberately fan through the face-down cards. Take out the first face-up card along with the card above it and set them on the table. Fan through to the next face-up card; remove it and the card above it, placing them next to the pair on the table.

Turn over each of the face-down cards, showing how wonderfully *simpatico* you two really are. Be sure to tell the spectator, "You really did a great job. I have a feeling you must be psychic."

Note: If you have performed *Three-Card Surprise* (page 35) and spectators ask for a repeat, you can do this one. The effect is similar, but the method, as you can see, is quite different.

If you decide to do this, do *not* indicate that you are going to produce the same effect. Instead, say, "Let me show you something a little different." Then proceed with the patter above.

Astounding Appearance

This trick lives up to its title. It's as close to real magic as you're ever going to get. Occasionally you'll come across someone who knows the basic trick; don't let that hold you back. If someone says, "Oh, I know that one," or, "I do that one myself," simply give the person a conspiratorial wink and continue. The effect is worth it.

A spectator chooses a card and replaces it in the deck, which is shuffled. You show four cards individually; none is the selected card. Again you show the four cards and place them in the spectator's hand. You take away three cards, snap your fingers, and the remaining card is the chosen one.

Here's how. First, force a card. Use *One-Cut Force* (page 19), *Face-Up Force* (page 19), or *Double-Turnover Force* (page 20). Have the card shown around and replaced in the deck. After the spectator shuffles the deck, fan through the cards, faces towards you, saying, "I'm not absolutely sure which one is yours, but I think I can locate it within four cards." Cut the deck so that the forced card is fourth from the bottom. The cut is done quite openly. "I'm sure you'll agree that narrowing it down to four cards is truly mediocre."

Before we proceed, check *The Glide* (page 24). Hold the deck in the glide grip and show the bottom card, asking, "Is this your card?" When the spectator says no, turn the deck down and deal the bottom card onto the table. Place the new bottom card on top of the deck without showing its face, remarking, "And we place the next card on top—for magical purposes." This is more effective than saying, "I place the next card on top because I feel like it." Or even worse, "I place the next card on top because if I don't, you'll soon be shown the same card twice in a row."

Tip the deck up, showing the new bottom card. "Is this your card?" Naturally, the spectator denies it. Turn the deck down and perform the glide, dealing the spectator's chosen card onto the one on the table. Place the bottom card (the one you just showed the spectator) on top of the deck, repeating, "We place the next card on top—for magical purposes."

Show the bottom card and again ask if this is the chosen one. The spectator says no. As you place it on top of the two on the table, attempt to look crest-fallen. This time, when you place the bottom card on top (to be consistent), pause after you say, "I place the next card on top . . ." Eye the spectators questioningly; they will be happy to explain that you are doing this for magical purposes.

Repeat the whole business, placing the bottom card on top of the three on the table and the new bottom card on top. When the spectator denies that the fourth one is his card, ask, "Are you sure?" Look puzzled, unless puzzlement is your natural look— in which case, look natural. "Now let's check to make sure."

There is now a pile of four cards on the table; the second one from the bottom is the chosen card. Pick up the pile and hold the cards in the glide grip. Ask the spectator to hold out his hand.

Show the bottom card. "This isn't yours?" you query. Of course he responds negatively. Turn the pile downwards and perform the glide, placing the spectator's chosen card face down on his extended palm. Place the next card on top for magical purposes.

Show the bottom card, repeating the query. Turn the pile down and place the bottom card on the spectator's palm. Do *not* shift a card to the top. Fan the remaining two cards, showing them to the spectator with the question, "And neither one of these is yours?" Add these to the face-down cards in the spectator's hand.

"Now let's check this again." Take the top card from the pile in the spectator's hand. Place it face up in your other hand, saying, "This isn't yours?" Quickly take the second card, place it face up on the first card you took, and repeat the question. And once more with the third card. Place the three cards to one side. Remaining in his hand is the chosen card.

To prevent premature disclosure, take his other hand and place it on top of the card. "Hold the card right there, please. Now tell me, what's the name of your card?" Gently hold his hand on the card so that he doesn't show it yet.

When he names his card, snap your fingers over his hands and then gesture to him, indicating that he should turn the card over.

Note: The key to this trick is performing it with some speed. No doubt you have noticed that when you place the cards in the spectator's hand, you show the same card twice. Don't worry about it— even when it is an obvious card, like an ace. If you proceed apace, no one will notice. I have done the trick for many, many years, and nobody has ever called me on it.

Murder

Here's a very simple trick I came up with many years ago. It's one of those story tricks that spectators usually enjoy, and it has a surprise ending.

Put the four queens in a face-up row on the table. Also, lay the four aces, a king, and a jack to one side, also face up. A spectator selects a card and places it face up near the queens. Take the jack and place it next to the chosen card. Then use the following patter.

"I hope you all enjoy murder mysteries. The one I am about to present is challenging, thrilling, exciting, and preposterous. See if you can solve the murders. Yes, I said *murders*; this is going to be a juicy one. Now these four queens are rich, old spinsters living alone in a huge mansion. You, as symbolized by the six of clubs (name the chosen card), are their lawyer and in charge of their finances." Nod knowingly. Obviously, the spectator will be a prime suspect.

"One night you are visiting the four ladies. Also in the house is the tall, gaunt, old butler. Indicate the jack. You notice that from time to time he glares maniacally at the old ladies.

"Suddenly the lights go out, there is a shot (snap your fingers), and when the lights go on again, one of the ladies has been murdered." Turn one of the queens face down.

"You are a good friend of the chief of police (indicate the king), so you phone him and ask for help. He immediately sends out four of his best detectives to surround the house." Put the four aces in a face-up square around the queens, the jack, and the chosen card.

"If the detectives had been sensible, they would have gone *inside* the house. But that might have prevented any more murders, and would have spoiled this engrossing murder mystery. Somehow they must have known that.

"Sure enough, the lights went out, a shot was fired (snap your fingers), and another lady was murdered." Turn down another queen.

"Before the detectives could get to the house, the lights went out again, and two shots rang out (snap your fingers twice), and both remaining ladies were murdered." Turn the last two queens face down.

"The chief was infuriated when he learned of this, so he came to the house personally and gathered up all the suspects and took them to the station for a lie detector test." Gather up the cards so that they will read, from top to bottom: chosen card, ace, ace, jack, ace, ace.

"Yes, the chief was even suspicious of his own detectives. For the lie detector test, he decided to use the word 'murder.' Whoever reacted positively to his word would be the guilty party. So let's spell out 'murder.' "

See *The Glide* (page 24). Hold the cards in your left hand in the glide grip and transfer one card from the top to the bottom for each letter as you spell out the word "murder." Show the ace at the bottom. Turn the cards face down and deal the ace face down on the table with the right fingers.

"We eliminate one of the detectives." Repeat the spelling, and the chosen card appears at the bottom. Show this card as before, but when you turn the cards down, perform the glide, drawing off the second card from the bottom and placing it face down on top of the ace you have eliminated.

"And—surprise!—you too are eliminated." Continue the elimination until only two cards remain.

"This leaves only two suspects: one of the ace detectives and the butler. Naw, it couldn't be the butler."

As you say this, separate the two cards, holding one face down in each hand. When you bring them back together, put the former bottom one on top. Spell out "murder" again. Show the bottom card, the jack, and deal it into the elimination pile.

"I *knew* it couldn't be the butler. So who do we have left? That rotten, vicious, conniving, sneaky, criminal . . ."

Look at the remaining card.

"Oh, no. There must be some mistake."
Turn the chosen card face up.

Quaint Coincidence

This one should be reserved for times when you have two bright, cooperative spectators, helpers who are capable of following directions.

This is similar in some respects to *Tricky Transpo* (page 42), so it would not be advisable to perform both in the same set, but it is different enough to include here, since it has an excellent climax.

Hand the deck out to be shuffled. Turn your back and have one spectator think of an odd number from five to twenty-five. Another spectator thinks of an even number from five to twenty-five. Each spectator is to count off the number of cards equal to the number he thought of. The rest of the deck is put aside. The two piles are put together and shuffled.

Turn around and take the pile. Tell the two assistants to note the two cards that lie at the numbers they thought of. Once they have noted the cards, they need not remember the number. Slowly deal the cards into a face-up pile, counting aloud as you do so. When you complete the deal, pick up the cards and turn them face down.

"Now don't forget your cards," you smilingly caution, "or this effect goes right up in smoke. We've dealt the cards only once, and, as you know, three is the magic number. So let's try deal number two."

Before you deal, give the cards a false cut—see the *One-Finger Cut* (page 21)—to throw off spectators.

Now hold the cards face down in the left hand and, starting at your left, deal them alternately into two face-down piles.

"Now for the third and magical deal." Take the left-hand pile face up in your left hand, and the other face down in your right hand. "Stop me immediately if either of you sees his card."

Simultaneously thumb off cards into two piles. Deal from the top of each pile. Make sure that you have exactly the *same* number of cards in each pile. Clearly, the pile on your left is dealt face up and the one on your right, face down. When one of the spectators tells you to stop, set the cards in your hands aside. Point to the face-up card and ask the spectator if he is certain that it is his. Then ask the second spectator to name his card.

When he does so, turn over the top card of the other pile, revealing the quaint coincidence.

Illus. 14.   Try to conceal a card in the palm of your right hand.

Mind Reading

A Word About Mind Reading

There are three ways in which the card artist can read minds:

1. *Force* the selection of a card on a spectator.
2. Learn the name of a card after a spectator has thought of it.
3. Actually use telepathy.

If you can do number three, you may as well skip this section. Most often the mind reader uses method one. Four of the five tricks in this section are actually *forces*. Some might be applicable to other tricks where it is necessary for you to know the name of a selected card, but the *forces* on pages 18 through 20 are quicker and more direct. Obviously, you can decide for yourself.

If you are going to do mind reading, I recommend that you program a number of tricks. Besides the tricks in this section, you might choose among the various prediction tricks.

If you are doing several mind-reading tricks, a spectator might naturally wonder, "Why can't I just think of a card and then you name it?" Before the issue comes up, I like to explain, "I am better able to see the card in your mind if you actually look at a card and then concentrate as you visualize it." Sure, it's nonsense. But if you *can* read minds, it's semilogical. There will be more tips on the techniques of mind reading as you go along.

In the Palm of Your Hand

Don't be frightened by this one. It's as close as you can come to real mind reading.

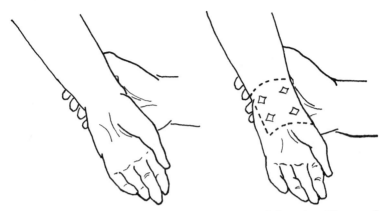

Illus. 15. Place your right hand on your left wrist. The card should now be completely hidden.

First, let's practise. Hold the deck in your left hand. Push off the top card and, with the aid of the left middle fingers, take it into the palm of your right hand, trying to conceal it (Illus. 14). Don't worry; I'm not going to ask you to palm a card in plain sight. Put the cards behind your back and try the same palm. Now place your right hand on your left wrist as in Illus. 15. Practise this a few times. You're ready to roll.

To start, you must know the top card. See *The Peek* (page 17). Now ask a spectator to come up and help you. For this trick, you cannot be surrounded by spectators, as you will see. Have the spectator stand by your side as you put your hands behind your back, deck in the left hand. Palm the top card and place your right hand on your wrist, as described above. Obviously, no one should be in a position to observe this.

Turn your back to the spectator, offering the deck, and say, "Cut off a pile of cards, please." After he has done so, turn towards him, add the palmed card to the top of the deck, and reclasp your wrist, saying, "Is that enough?" Again, no one can be behind you to observe.

The answer to your question is invariably yes. If he says no, say, "Sure, it is," and proceed. Turn your back to the spectator again and proffer the cards in your hand, saying, "Look at the card you cut to, show it around, and replace it."

After he has done this, say, "Now put the rest of the cards on top and take the deck."

Apparently, the spectator has cut the deck, looked at the card he cut to, and replaced the cutoff cards. What's more, he then took the deck into his own hands, eliminating the possibility of your trying any funny business.

Turn to face the spectator. It is time for a little psychological smoke screen. "I would like you to give the deck one complete shuffle." The spectator shuffles the deck.

"Aha!" say the spectators to themselves, "He must know the card above or below the selected card." They know a trick that works like that.

You continue to foster the misapprehension by saying, "Now if I go through the deck and find your card, would that be a good trick?" Usually the spectator agrees.

"Well, I don't want to do a trick. Instead, I am going to attempt to read your mind."

Take the deck from the spectator and hold it to your forehead. "Please concentrate on your card. I see red clouds. I would say your card is a red—a diamond. Let me see—it looks like a four—no, no—an ace. The ace of diamonds."

Equally, you could see dark clouds, of course, for a spade or a club. I like the idea of almost naming the wrong value, briefly mistaking a four for an ace, a queen for a jack, a three for an eight—any two cards that look somewhat alike. All of this enhances the illusion that you are actually mind-reading.

Crisscross

One piece of advice: Just because a trick is easy, don't give it short shrift. Just because the secret is simple, don't hurry through your presentation. A simple method of mind reading, for instance, can be just as effective as a complex one—maybe even more so. Consider this trick, which appears in most elementary magic books. When I teach magic, I use this to provide insight on presentation.

To begin with, you must know the top card of the deck. See *The Peek* (page 17). Set the deck down and ask a spectator to cut off a pile of cards. He is to set the pile down and put the rest of the deck on top of it crosswise.

The former top card of the deck is now on top of the lower pile; you know it, and if the spectators think about it, they know too. They aren't going to think about that, because you're going to do this absurdly simple trick like a real pro. You're going to take their minds and eyes off the cards.

To do this, you merely speak for a moment. I usually say something like this: "You had complete freedom of choice as to where you cut the cards. You could have cut off a big pile, a little pile, whatever you chose. Now I want you to take a look at your card." Here you *touch* the card he is to look at so there will be no mistake (Illus. 16).

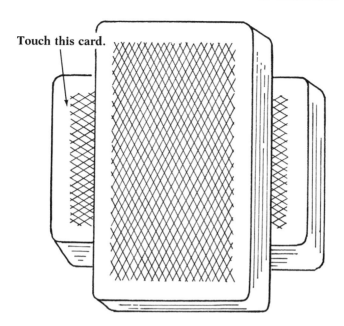

Touch this card.

Illus. 16. The spectator cuts off a pile of cards, sets down the deck, and then places the rest of the deck on top of it, crosswise. Then, touch the top card of the lower pile with your forefinger.

You do *not* say, "I want you to look at the card you cut to." This might bring up nasty thoughts, like, "Which one *did* I cut to?"

Have him show the card around. Now add more tinsel to the tree by having him replace the card from where he took it and even up the deck. He is to give the deck one shuffle of his choice, but only one shuffle.

Again, you hold the deck to your forehead and gradually reveal the color, the suit, and the value.

Yes, the trick is elementary. So what? Does it fool people? With proper presentation, it certainly does. Toss this in occasionally among the more subtle mind-reading tricks and check out the spectator re-action. I think you'll be pleased.

The Big Deal

To begin with, you must know the second card from the bottom of the deck. You may choose among the methods offered in *The Peek* (page 17). I recommend this variation of number four.

You say, "The vibes just aren't right. I'd better remove my bad-luck card."

As you fan through the deck, note the second card from the bottom. Continue on to the queen of spades, or some other "bad luck" card, and remove it from the deck. If you can, shuffle the deck, retaining at least the bottom two cards.

Hold the cards in the left hand in the dealing position, with the thumb along the left edge (Illus. 17). Run the thumb down the side of the deck, riffling all the cards. Do this a few times and then say,

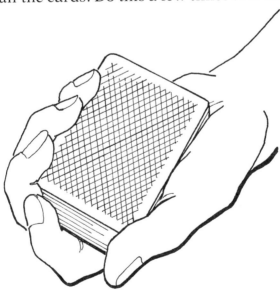

Illus. 17. Hold the cards in your left hand, in the dealing position, with your thumb along the left edge.

"I want you to select a card. Just tell me when to stop as I riffle through."

Now the spectator is going to get the bottom portion of the deck, and you want him to have less than half the cards. So start your riffle just above the middle, and riffle *slowly*. Make sure you stop *exactly* where the spectator indicates. Keep the top portion and give the bottom portion to the spectator.

"Now let's deal them into piles, one card at a time." Deal your pile in front of you, as he deals his in front of him. Match him card for card. Stop dealing when the spectator runs out of cards. Set the rest of your cards aside.

Tell the spectator, "Place your top card in the middle. Now put your bottom card in the middle. Next, look at the new top card and show it around."

Suiting action to words, you have shown the spectator the way by placing the top card in the middle of your pile and the bottom card in the middle of your pile. You have also lifted the top card of your pile, *definitely not looking at it*, and returned it to the top. The card the spectator has looked at is, of course, the card which was originally the second card from the bottom of the deck.

Tell the spectator to shuffle his packet. Hand him your packet and tell him to shuffle it in with the others. It is a mistake, I believe, to simply name the chosen card. I like to stress the mind reading. Granted, there may be a hint of a twinkle in my eye. While it is true that the spectators, at one level, *know* you cannot possibly read minds, it is just possible that you may be able to. And how *could* you have done it if you had not read the spectator's mind?

I tell the spectator to concentrate on his card as he shuffles. Then, as with the other mind-reading tricks, I gradually reveal the suit and the value.

Pretend to concentrate. You might tell the spectator something like this: "You may or may not believe in mind reading, but I would like you to do as I ask. Please concentrate on the color of your card. Actually think of the color." Then reveal the color.

"Now please think of the suit." As you concentrate, tell the spectator that you are getting mixed signals, that you can't be quite sure. Then tell him the suit. Do something similar in revealing the value.

Believe me, all of this razzmatazz enhances the trick. The spectators are not quite sure whether you have actually performed mind reading. Regardless, they know you have done a great trick.

The Three Piles

I invented this trick by combining two well-known principles. You will like this one, I think, when, after you have finished, you hear spectators comment on how "you didn't even touch the cards."

Again, you must know the top card. You can use one of the methods listed under *The Peek* (page 17). Then, if you can, shuffle the cards, making sure that the top card stays there.

Hand the deck to a spectator and tell him to deal out a pile. After he has dealt seven or eight cards, tell him to stop when he feels like it. Ask him to deal another pile next to it. Again, after several cards have been dealt, tell him to stop when he wishes. Tell him to deal a third pile next to the second one. When the spectator has finished dealing to the third pile, take the rest of the cards from him and set them aside.

The spectator now has three piles in front of him. The *bottom* card of the first pile he dealt is the original top card of the deck.

Tell the spectator, "Put your hand on a pile, please."

1. If he places his hand on the first pile he dealt, gather up the two remaining piles, placing them on top of the deck. Tell him to look at the bottom card of his pile.

2. If he places his hand on a different pile, say, "And place your other hand on a pile."

Suppose he places his *other* hand on a different pile. Don't *say* anything. Gesture with your two hands that he is to hand you the two piles he is covering. If he doesn't catch on, say, "Hand me the two piles, please." Put the two piles on top of the deck and tell the spectator to look at the bottom card of his pile.

Suppose he places his *other* hand on the pile containing the force card. Pick up the uncovered pile. Tell the spectator, "Lift a hand, please."

If he lifts the hand covering the pile containing the force card, gesture that he is to hand you the covered pile. If his eyes glaze over, point to the covered pile and say, "Hand me the pile, please." Have him look at the bottom card of the remaining pile.

If he lifts his other hand, the covered pile is the one containing the force card. Pick up the uncovered pile and have him look at the bottom card of the remaining pile.

The above *sounds* complicated, but just run through it a few times and you will find that, in practice, it is quite simple.

After the spectator has looked at the bottom card of the pile and has shown the card around, have him place the pile (with the chosen card) on top of the deck. Even up the deck and set it aside. Then, as with the previous three effects, read the spectator's mind as convincingly as you can.

The Three Location

The previous mind-reading tricks were variations of forcing a card on a spectator. This trick, however, is quite different.

Since I first came across *The Three Location* many years ago, I have included it nearly every time I have displayed my so-called mental powers. In the original version, the spectator was offered only nine cards to choose from. As a slight improvement, I developed a method of offering thirteen cards.

Fan through the deck, saying, "I want to find a suitable card for you to choose mentally." Find a three, count six cards beyond it, and cut the cards at that point so that the three becomes the seventh card from the top.

"I'm going to show you some cards, and I want you to think of one. I won't watch your face, and I don't want you to say anything when you have thought of one."

Slowly show the cards one by one to the spectator, taking them one under the other so that they remain in the same order. Keep your head averted. Show the spectator exactly thirteen cards and return them to the top, saying, "Do you have one?"

If his answer is no, say, "I'll go slower this time," and go through the thirteen cards again. When the spectator has one, say, "Now I'll try to find your card."

Put the deck behind your back, count off six cards and turn the seventh card (the three you found) face up. Replace the six cards on top, cut the deck, and bring the cards forward.

"I have located your card in the deck. What's the name of your card?" If he names the three, you have a miracle. Show him that it is face up in the middle.

If it is another card, fan through the cards, faces towards you, saying, "Note that there is a face-up card in the middle." As you fan to the three, showing the face-up card, spread the cards on either side, so that you can see where the chosen card is in relation to it.

Turn the cards face down, leaving them spread out. If his card is either directly above or below the three, say, "And with the face-up card, I have located your card." Pull out the face-up three with the chosen card, either above or below it. "What's the name of your card?" you ask. The spectator repeats the name. Turn the two cards over, revealing the mentally selected card.

If his chosen card is second from the three on either side, say, "Note that the face-up card is a three." In fact, you make this statement in all ensuing instances. Now you start on the three and count to the selected card, like this: Touch the three, saying, "One"; touch the second card, saying, "Two"; touch the selected card, saying, "Three." Pull the selected card from the deck. As before, and in all other instances, ask, "What is the name of your card?" When he repeats the name, turn the card over.

If the thought-of card is three cards from the three on either side, count over three, as above, starting with the *next* card. Pull the selected card from the deck, and finish as before.

Suppose his selected card is four cards from the three. As before, say, "Note that the face-up card is a three." Then, starting with the three, spell out T-H-R-E-E, landing on his selected card.

If the selected card is five cards from the three, spell out T-H-R-E-E, starting with the card next to your face-up three, again landing on his selected card.

If it is six cards from the three, again spell out T-H-R-E-E, starting with the card next to your face-up three, but, at the completion of your spelling, pull out the *next* card.

Why do you ask the spectator to name his card twice? Nothing but good can come of it. It helps build to the climax. Also, some spectators will forget that you asked the first time; thus, you have a genuine miracle. What's more, you create the impression that you paid no attention when the thought-of card was named the first time.

When you fan the cards, showing the face-up three to the spectators, they see only the backs of the cards and they are looking at the face-up card you are displaying. They do not realize that at the same time, you are looking at the faces of the cards.

Despite my labored explanation, this is quite a snappy trick. Need I add, do it only once?

ODDS AND
ENDS

Whoops!

The trick has gone perfectly up to now. The spectator names his card. You are holding a card in your hand. Nothing would afford you greater pleasure than that this should be the one named. But it is not.

Don't give up. "Sorry, I screwed up," is not really a great climax to a trick. Here are three alternatives. You can end up either a semiwinner or a total winner.

1. Don't ever reveal the card until after the spectator names it. This not only makes for a better climax, but also can help with an "out." For instance, the spectator names his card. You look at the one in your hand, nod, and say, "That's right." Bury the card in the deck and add, "Want to see another one?" Regardless, proceed with your next trick.

This isn't great, but it usually produces a chuckle rather than murmurs of sympathy.

2. Turn the card over, saying, "Wrong. It's the queen of hearts." Reassure him, "It's probably not all your fault." Or again: "Want to see another?"

3. Turn over the wrong card and say in your best voice, "Not only have I brought your card to the top, but I have also caused it to magically change to the queen of hearts." Pause. "Want to see it again?"

I use this as a rescue on occasion, and sometimes as a regular "trick."

4. When you get the bad news, show the card. *Instantly* turn it face down and hand it to the spectator, saying, "We're going to need this card in a moment." Hold the deck up so that only you can see the faces. Remark, "I want to check and make sure your card is still here and that I didn't accidentally slip it into my pocket."

Fan through the cards, starting at the bottom. After you have fanned through several cards, murmur, "No," and transfer them to the top in a bunch. Fan several more cards and transfer them to the top in the same way. Continue until you come to the chosen card. Put the cards below it on top; the card is now on the bottom.

"I can't find it," you say. "Let's see if you have better luck." Set the deck on the table. Cut off a small packet and place it next to the deck. Say, "Tell me when to stop."

Continue cutting off small packets and placing them on top of the original small packet until the spectator tells you to stop. Tell him to place the card he holds face up on *either* pile.

If he places it on the original deck, tell him to cut that pile and complete the cut. This places the face-up card and the chosen card face-to-face. He is then to place that pile on the other. You then invite as many additional complete cuts as desired.

If he places the card face up on the accumulated packets, indicate that he should place the original deck on top of that pile. Again, the face-up card and the chosen card are face-to-face. The deck may be given as many complete cuts as desired.

Fan through the cards and remove from the deck the face-up card and the card facing it (the chosen card). Once more, ask the spectator to name his card. When he does, turn the chosen card over, showing that he found his own card. You can comment, "Well, you had better luck than I did."

5. Once again, you have the wrong card. Show it, return it to the deck, and say, "Are you sure the five of spades was your card?" As before, fan through the cards so that no one else can see the faces. Again, place small groups on top until you come to the chosen card. Cut the cards at that point so that the chosen card comes to the top. Turn the deck face down, saying, "I must have missed it."

Now you can "discover" his card in a variety of ways. You might, for example, choose one of the forces provided in the section *Nothing Up My Sleeve* (page 15). You may choose to use another trick to reveal the card. For instance, the latter part of *Ups and Downs* (page 58) would be perfect. Simply complete the trick from the point where you have the spectator's card on top of the deck. Other tricks can be used in this way.

Missing the first time does not have to be fatal. Jugglers and acrobats frequently miss the first time just to build suspense. If you proceed confidently after a miss, spectators may well assume that it's all part of the show.

Parting Thoughts _____

Write It Down

Go through the tricks again and jot down the page numbers of the ones you particularly like. When you finish, try out your selections—first on yourself, and then on others. It is easy to get into the habit of performing certain favorites, and letting other excellent tricks fade from memory. You can prevent this by keeping a record right from the beginning.

When you find a good card trick, perhaps you should make a memorandum of it—jot some notes down on a file card or in a notebook. From time to time, you can consult your notes and freshen up your routines.

Simplify

Some say that the perfect trick is one that has been simplified to the point that it requires no sleight of hand. I don't know about that, but I believe that you *should* try to simplify every trick as much as possible. Do you really need all those sleights? Can you substitute subtlety for a sleight, or simply drop one altogether? Think it through. At least in some respect, every trick you do should be uniquely yours.

Stay Within Yourself

You have heard the expression, usually in sports, that a certain person should "stay within himself." For instance, if a player tries to do too much, he will probably mess up altogether. Similarly, when you do card tricks, you should stay within yourself. Don't try tricks you haven't mastered. Don't experiment with sleights in public. Practise in private until the sleight is perfected. Why risk exposure when there are so many tricks that you do perfectly?

Be Prepared

Should you carry a deck of cards with you wherever you go? Although this may not be a bad idea, what you should *definitely* know is what you're going to do when someone hands you a deck.

It's quite simple, really. It doesn't matter whether you're at a party, in a small group, or with an individual—your response is the same. Have in mind three or four tricks that are particularly effective and that you perform especially well. The tricks need not be related or sequential—just *good*.

Suppose these tricks are well received and you are encouraged to do more. *Now* you're ready to perform a routine. The makeup of this program is your choice, of course. It can consist of all gambling tricks or all mental tricks, for example. Personally, I prefer variety. Whatever you decide, perform no more than five or six tricks, closing with one of your best, a guaranteed eyepopper.

About the Author _____

Bob Longe, a retired English teacher, is an ardent hobbyist. He has charted stocks, played duplicate bridge, and painted. He plays the piano, the tenor banjo, and the ukulele. Inspired by the big stage shows of the great illusionists Blackstone and Dante, he took up magic in the 1930s. He wrote two booklets on card tricks: *The Invisible Deck* was published by the Ireland Magic Company of Chicago; *The Visible Deck* was self-published. Over the years, he has taught magic, particularly card tricks and coin tricks, to dozens of aspiring magicians.

In the late 1970s, Bob wrote, coproduced, and performed in the syndicated radio satire show, "Steve Sado, Private Eye." He lives in Rochester Hills, Michigan, with his wife, Betty.

Mastery Levels Chart & Index

Card Trick	P.	Easy	Harder	Advanced
Ace Surprise	83		★	
Astounding Appearance	99			★
Behind My Back	53		★	
Big Deal	112			★
Colorful Prediction	33		★	
Countdown	85	★		
Crisscross	110	★		
Digital Estimation	46			★
Do-It-Yourself Discovery	52	★		
Double-Match Trick	97		★	
Double-Turnover Force	20	★		
Easy Aces	40	★		
Easy Estimation	44	★		
Face-Up Force	19	★		
Flush of Success	78			★
Four Aces Again	86		★	
Gambling Aces	81		★	
Get Out of This World	88			★
Glide	24			★
Hot Spell	70	★		
Impromptu Speller	62		★	
In the Palm of Your Hand	107		★	
Mind Control Poker	75			★
Murder	102			★
My Favorite Card	57	★		
One-Cut Force	19	★		
One-Finger Cut	21		★	
Peek	17	★		
Perfect Pile	49			★

Mastery Levels Chart & Index

Card Trick	P.	Easy	Harder	Advanced
Presto Prediction	29		★	
Process of Elimination	94		★	
Quaint Coincidence	105		★	
Quick Speller	64			★
Rare Reverse	54		★	
Three-Card Surprise	35			★
Three Location	116			★
Three Piles	114		★	
Tick Tock Trick	39	★		
Tricky Transpo	42		★	
Two-Handed Poker	73	★		
Ups and Downs	58		★